General editor: Graham Handley M

Brodie's Notes on Aldous Huxley's

Brave New World

Graham Handley MA Ph.D.
Formerly Principal Lecturer in English, College of All Saints, Tottenham

MACMILLAN

First published by James Brodie Ltd
This revised edition first published 1990
by Pan Books Ltd

Reprinted 1992 by
THE MACMILLAN PRESS LTD
Houndmills, Basingstoke, Hampshire RG21 2XS
and London
Companies and representatives
throughout the world

ISBN 0-333-58129-6

Printed in Great Britain by
Clays Ltd, St Ives plc, Bungay, Suffolk

Contents

States of Utopia would appear to be more within reach than we believed before. And we, in reality, find ourselves facing a question which would otherwise be alarming. How do we avoid their definitive realization? Utopias are possible. Life is moving towards Utopias. And perhaps a new age is beginning, an age in which intellectuals and the educated classes will dream of means to avoid Utopias and return to a non-Utopian society, less 'perfect' and more free.

(Translated from the French of Nikolas Berdiaeff)

Berdiaeff, Nikolas (1874–1948, who wrote the extract, translated, which appears at the front of Huxley's novel), Russian idealist philosopher, student of Karl Marx, he welcomed the Russian revolution, but was later dismissed and went to Berlin. He believed in messianic nationalism with a claim for church unity.

Preface

The intention throughout this study aid is to stimulate and guide, to encourage your involvement in the book, and to develop informed responses and a sure understanding of the main details.

Brodie's Notes provide a clear outline of the play or novel's plot, followed by act, scene, or chapter summaries and/or commentaries. These are designed to emphasize the most important literary and factual details. Poems, stories or non-fiction texts combine brief summary with critical commentary on individual aspects or common features of the genre being examined. Textual notes define what is difficult or obscure and emphasize literary qualities. Revision questions are set at appropriate points to test your ability to appreciate the prescribed book and to write accurately and relevantly about it.

In addition, each of these Notes includes a critical appreciation of the author's art. This covers such major elements as characterization, style, structure, setting and themes. Poems are examined technically – rhyme, rhythm, for instance. In fact, any important aspect of the prescribed work will be evaluated. The aim is to send you back to the text you are studying.

Each study aid concludes with a series of general questions which require a detailed knowledge of the book: some of these questions may invite comparison with other books, some will be suitable for coursework exercises, and some could be adapted to work you are doing on another book or books. Each study aid has been adapted to meet the needs of the current examination requirements. They provide a basic, individual and imaginative response to the work being studied, and it is hoped that they will stimulate you to acquire disciplined reading habits and critical fluency.

Graham Handley 1990

The author and his work

Aldous Huxley was born in 1894. His father was the son of the distinguished T. H. Huxley, scientist and man of letters, and his mother was the granddaughter of Dr Arnold of Rugby and the niece of Matthew Arnold, poet and critic. His early family life with his brothers Julian and Trevenen appears to have been happy, and there is abundant evidence of a sensitivity, alertness and intelligence beyond his years. In 1900 his father, who had been a master at Charterhouse, became assistant editor of the Cornhill magazine, and the family moved to Prior's Field; there, in 1902, Mrs Huxley founded a school, which subsequently prospered.

Aldous, who was devoted to his mother, attended the school for a time, then went on to preparatory school and Eton in 1908. At the end of November in that year his mother died; Aldous, grief-stricken, later returned to Eton where, in 1911, he contracted a disease of the eyes which reduced him to semi-blindness. As a result, he had to leave Eton, but he taught himself to read braille, to type and to play the piano. His sight began to recover after a year or so, and later he could read sufficiently well to go up to Balliol College, Oxford. In 1914 he tried to enlist, but was rejected because of his eyes. In 1915 he met D. H. Lawrence for the first time, and began to write verse; later he took a first-class honours degree in English, just as his mother Julia had done many years before. He spent much time at Garsington during the war, where Lady Ottoline Morell and her husband Philip encouraged and employed many conscientious objectors; he met, among others, T. S. Eliot and Virginia Woolf, and he fell in love with a Belgian girl, Maria Nys, whom he subsequently married. He then taught at Eton, but he was not a success and chafed at the experience. He had continued to write, and in 1919 joined the staff of the weekly magazine *The Athenaeum*, which was then edited by John Middleton Murry. At this time he wrote reviews, articles and poems at a great rate. *Limbo* (short stories) was published in 1920, and this was followed by a book of verse called *Leda*. His first novel, somewhat after the style and method of Thomas Love Peacock (1786–1866), was *Crome*

Yellow, which appeared late in 1921. It was cynically interpreted for the most part, and many people, including Huxley's own family, were shocked; more particularly the Morells, for Crome could be readily associated with Garsington.

The following year saw the publication of another book of stories, *Mortal Coils*, which contained the rightly celebrated 'The Gioconda Smile', which was later dramatized. In 1923 Huxley signed an agreement with the publishers Chatto & Windus which assured him a regular income provided, of course, that he supplied novels or stories or essays. His next work of fiction was *Antic Hay*, which reinforced the idea, through its picture of contemporary cultural and pseudo-cultural society, that Huxley was both sceptical and iconoclastic. The Huxleys spent most of the next four years in Italy, and during this time another book of stories, *Little Mexican*, and a novel, *Those Barren Leaves*, appeared. Then they set off for the East, and Aldous recorded his impressions, particularly of India, in the travel book *Jesting Pilate* (1926). At this time he was also publishing books of essays which displayed the individuality of his approach, his easy style and the breadth – and depth – of his erudition, as well as his infinite capacity to receive and to communicate impressions. In 1926 Huxley re-met D. H. Lawrence in Florence, and they spent some time together in 1928, when Huxley finished *Point Counter Point*, which became a bestseller. It was a portrait, cynical, racy, astute, of contemporary society and, as Sir Isaiah Berlin has rightly observed, it showed Huxley's ability to produce 'ideas so freely, so gaily, with such virtuosity'. He returned to London briefly in 1929, and *Point Counter Point* was dramatized in 1930, running for just eight weeks.

In 1930 D. H. Lawrence died, and Huxley began to collect his letters for an edition. *Brave New World* was written in four months in 1931 and was published in February 1932. Its impact in this country was immediate but, strangely, initially it was much less so in the United States. The collected edition of the *Letters of D. H. Lawrence* was published in 1932, *Eyeless in Gaza* in 1936, and *Ends and Means* in 1937. In 1938 the Huxleys moved to Hollywood and he submitted a film script on *Madame Curie* which was never used. He became increasingly worried about his sight, but studied and practised the Bates cure, which worked for him.

He was very upset by the war which began in 1939. October

1941 saw the publication of *Grey Eminence, A Study in Religion and Politics*, and this was followed by *The Art of Seeing* (1943), his own particular tribute to and investigation of the Bates method. *Science, Liberty and Peace* and *The Perennial Philosophy* were next, and in 1946 he adapted his own *The Gioconda Smile* for the cinema. *Ape and Essence* (1948), a frightening post-atomic novel, was succeeded by *The Devils of Loudun* and *The Genius and the Goddess*. In 1955 his wife died, and in 1956 he remarried, beginning *Island*, but abandoning it in the following year while he wrote the series of essays which constitute *Brave New World Revisited* (1958). In 1960 he became seriously ill; in 1961 he continued to work on *Island*, his contrasting, optimistic look into the future; and his house and all his books and papers were destroyed by fire in that year. In 1962 *Island* was finally published, while *Literature and Science* appeared in 1963. In October/ November of that year he wrote *Shakespeare and Religion*, his last work and died, virtually unnoticed, on 22 November 1963; on that day John Fitzgerald Kennedy, President of the United States, was assassinated. This coincidence could be seen as a final irony; for Huxley, who was prophet, humanist, scientist, man of literature and the arts, died in the shadow of a politician, Controller of the Western ideal, the leading representative of a brave new world which, like Huxley's, drew its being from a scientific base – the atom bomb, the space capsule, the immeasurable capacity of man to diminish man in his advance into the nuclear age.

The outline above can give little indication of the quality of the man himself, and the student is directed towards one of the outstanding biographies of our time, Sybille Bedford's two-volume study of Huxley (Chatto & Windus in association with Collins, 1973–4). A very interesting study of Huxley's work, with some cogent comments on *Brave New World, Island* and *Brave New World Revisited*, is to be found in George Woodcock's *Dawn and the Darkest Hour: A Study of Aldous Huxley* (Faber and Faber 1972). Certainly, any student of *Brave New World* should read *Ape and Essence* and *Island* in order to compare these with the first written, and George Orwell's futuristic novel *1984* has often been considered in the light of Huxley's work.

Title and source

The title of Huxley's novel, and it is repeated with ironic emphasis in the text by John, is taken from Miranda's words (*The Tempest* Act V Scene i) when Alonso, father to Ferdinand, interrupts the lovers as they are playing chess. By this stage in the play Prospero, Miranda's father, is bent on exercising his powers of forgiveness and reconciliation, so that he has agreed to the betrothal of Ferdinand and his daughter and forgiven Alonso for his part in his banishment. Miranda's words are as guileless as John's, but she too is speaking of what appears to be 'beauteous', although we know that in reality it is corrupt. If Huxley's title is examined closely, we shall find that there are other echoes of the plot of *The Tempest* which reflect how deeply he had studied the text and how saturated he was with its associations. There is a real Savage in *The Tempest*, Caliban, who tries to violate Miranda, but he too has his moments of poetry, one of which is quoted by Mustapha Mond to John; there is a controller in the sense that Prospero is a controller of the destinies of all who come within his orbit; the island is enchanted, and there is the *soma* enchantment of *Brave New World*; and there is the corruption of human nature, reflected in the court life and the ousting of Prospero, as compared with the scientific corruption (it amounts to that) of human nature in *Brave New World*. Doubtless other parallels could be found between the two works in terms of character and themes in particular, but another source for Huxley's work is the *Utopia* of Sir Thomas More (1478–1535); the word is taken from the Greek meaning 'nowhere', and it describes an imaginary island where everything is perfect – the laws, the morals and the politics, for example. It will be obvious that Huxley is writing an anti-Utopian study, since the perfection is synthetic and not human or intellectual; but he would be aware of the Utopia tradition and its offshoots – one should mention *Gulliver's Travels*, Samuel Butler's *Erewhon* and some of the writings of H. G. Wells, who was apparently not impressed by *Brave New World*. Huxley often looked to the future, and despite the pessimism and fears inherent in this novel and in *Brave New World*

Revisited (1958), the novel *Island* (1962) posits a fundamentally optimistic view of what could happen in spiritual and social terms in the years to come.

Plot, themes and structure

The narration in *Brave New World* is straightforward. It opens in the year AF 632 in the Central London Hatchery and Conditioning Centre, with the Director conducting a group of students on a tour of learning inspection; in effect, it is an introductory study of the basic conditioning of the world's populace in embryonic form, from Alphas to Epsilons, the complete range of society. Central to the conception of uniformity is the Bokanovsky process, whereby a maximum of ninety-six identical twins can be produced – all capable of doing exactly the same work and consequently of achieving the same socially acceptable results. The author's tone is ironic but at the same time meticulously scientific, all the detailed steps in the conditioning of the embryo being explained. The emphasis is on facts and figures, both from the Director and Henry Foster, since independent judgement and thought have been conditioned out of existence and detail is computerized to the point of demonstrating, for example, how many females emerge as deliberately sterile (i.e. freemartins).

Conditioning is for future environment, for employment in a strictly class-conscious, differentiated society, and its inception is in the nurseries, or the Neo-Pavlovian conditioning rooms, as they are called. The demonstrations are simple and effective – the children are taught to hate flowers and books, for example, by a series of alarm-bells and electric shocks, for as the D.H.C. observes, 'A love of nature keeps no factories busy', hence the decision to 'abolish the love of nature'. 'Parent' is a dirty word; in this way of life there is no family unit as such, for babies are 'decanted'. Children are further conditioned by 'hypnopaedia', sleep-teaching through microphones placed under their pillows while they are asleep. Then the students observe the children at their 'rudimentary sexual' games, and are told of how any display of sexuality in children was regarded as abnormal before the time of 'Our Ford'.

At this stage Huxley introduces an interesting, interacting structural device. Mustapha Mond, the Resident Controller for Western Europe, now appears and proceeds to fill in a number of historical gaps for the edification of the students (and, of course, the readers); but interspersed with his fragmentary accounts is a shift of emphasis which introduces us to Bernard Marx (note the name) of the Psychology Bureau, and Lenina Crowne and her friend Fanny, whose conversation takes place largely in the Girls' Dressing Room. There is a subtle linking of these three areas of attention: Mustapha Mond's account of the primitive times of the past includes mention of mother, home and family, while Lenina and Fanny discuss the use of the Pregnancy Substitute which has, artificially, scientifically, replaced the reality of birth. The organization of the plot here is skilful indeed, for the alternations are from the past to the present, from the closeness of the family to the 'everyone belongs to everyone else' of the 'hypnopaedic proverb'; and additionally, though never in the first person, there are telling interjections into the Mond account by the author himself which underline his own sympathetic identification with a way of life which involves feeling, suffering and solitude.

To be conventional means to be promiscuous by our standards; stability is the key to society, so that the machinery must always continue and the population must 'consume' goods. [A reflection on contemporary consumerism is seen to be epitomized by the USA.] This society has reversed the morality by which we live, and this is one of Huxley's basic themes: that ultimately man will be the slave of machines, that the individuality and imagination of man will die as a result, and that love will give way to lust and self-indulgence. Initially Bernard Marx, however, is not promiscuous, and has a romantic interest in – one might call it love for – Lenina Crowne, who returns his interest up to a point and has been invited by Bernard to go to a Savage Reservation. The fragmentary nature of the narrative, with Mond's emphasis on the elimination of feeling and suffering in the past set alongside Bernard's and Lenina's reactions in the present, is very effective – feeling, it seems, has not been removed entirely by conditioning. Also grafted into the narrative at this stage are the clichés of hypnopaedia, like 'ending is better than mending', and here single lines in alternation produce a strangely hypnotic effect, almost as if the techniques of hypnopaedia itself are being directed to the reader – a sufficient number of repetitions will carry him into this brave new world.

This world is a world state; the worship of Ford (or Freud, as he sometimes called himself) has replaced the worship of God; and Bernard Marx, whose reactions are revealed to us, is an odd man out. The movement of the plot by the end of Chapter 3 is considerable; we have been given a history in potted form of the destruction of civilization and culture as we know it in the 20th century, and at the same time we have been introduced to Bernard Marx and Lenina Crowne who do not appear, in their conscious reactions at least, to be quite the conventional Alphas they should be. And last, but most significant of all, we learn that everyone is addicted to *soma*, the drug that changes life into a dream, with the grades of dream-escape, so to speak, dependent on the number of tablets you take – an unlimited quantity per person being prescribed by the world state. The fabric of society having been established, we now move to the personal – Bernard, brooding and introspective, arranging to see Lenina (who is currently being 'had' by Henry Foster); the principle of the need to 'consume' is seen in the account of Lenina and Henry going off to play obstacle golf at Stoke Poges. The next character of importance to appear is Helmholtz Watson, lecturer at the College of Emotional Engineering, a man of like sympathies to Bernard, the embodiment of one of the main themes in the novel; despite the most rigorous conditioning, the survival of individual characteristics, of man's unconquerable need for identity and self-expression, will go on. Helmholtz's job, among other things, is to write the jingles and scripts which ensure the stability of the state. He is not merely different, like Bernard; he is physically attractive, is an Alpha Plus, has pride and integrity and a questioning mind.

He is seen in contrast – and part of the structure of *Brave New World* is a sense of balance and contrast which runs throughout – with Henry Foster, the complete conformist, who gives Lenina an account of phosphorous reclamation from the dead, as they return from Stoke Poges on their way to the Westminster Abbey cabaret. Again the use of contrast is employed. Lenina and Henry dance, are 'bottled' on *soma* and go back to Henry's apartment, with Lenina remembering to take the requisite contraceptive precautions; Bernard's experience is of a like nature but supposedly more heightened. He goes to the Fordson Community Singery, an ecstatically 'religious' ceremony (with strong Christian parallels and overtones), with *soma* again providing the thoroughly predictable and acceptable identification of man and Ford. 'The incarnation of the Greater Being', as it is called, is really a form of hysteria engendered by *soma*, and it ends with the frenzied ritual of 'orgy-porgy'. The satire, the irony (see the section on 'Style') are evident, and Huxley is commenting on the mob-hysteria present in his own time (in Italy, for example, where he lived for a time) and anticipating what was to come in the Germany of Adolf Hitler. But Bernard, although he conforms and pretends, is really outside the experience, and continues moody and different when he goes out with Lenina, wanting to be with her for reasons other than sexual ones. His weakness (he is seen in contrast with Helmholtz here) is that he succumbs to *soma* and enjoys the 'pneumatic' attractions of Lenina, although the following day he is stricken by remorse and unhappiness.

Bernard gets permission to go to the New Mexico Reservation with Lenina, and once again Huxley employs a retrospective technique (used earlier with Mustapha Mond) to integrate the past into the main fabric of the plot; the Director reminisces and tells Bernard of his own trip to the Reservation some twenty-five years before. This prepares us for the discovery of Linda and John later on and also for the subsequent exposure of the Director when they are brought to London by Bernard. Again the irony is present, since Bernard the unconventional is a little shocked at the Director's revelations of himself (he who is a stickler for conventionality, so much so that he pinched Lenina's bottom). The Director, aware that he has betrayed weakness, reprimands Bernard for his shortcomings and threatens to have him transferred to Iceland. Bernard is human enough to be elated by this reaction.

The next sequence in the structure of the plot is set in the Reservation, where Bernard and Lenina have everything explained to them by the Warden. Bernard, away from the stability of the society he knows, telephones Helmholtz (he realizes he has left his eau-de-Cologne tap in the bathroom running) and is appalled and terrified to hear that the Director has publicly announced that he (Bernard) is to be transferred to Iceland. Two grammes of *soma* provide the cushioned oblivion he needs, and he spends the night in the rest-house with Lenina. Later they are conducted to the *pueblo* by a native guide; Lenina has to experience dirt, and is horrified and affronted by the sight of the decrepitude of old age, babies feeding at the breast, and Bernard's deliberate – and somewhat affected – praise of the 'revoltingly viviparous scene'. The presence of a dead dog and a woman suffering from goitre further nauseate her. The parallelism in the plot is now emphasized, for Bernard and Lenina watch a ritual dance and initiation ceremony; this, unlike the simulated ecstasy of 'orgy-porgy', is real, involving as it does the beating of a boy and the compulsively symbolic shedding of blood in order, in part at least, to promote the growth of the crops. But as with the Solidarity Service, there are Christian overtones, with the boy having a Christ-like significance, and the three women who come to carry him in approximating to the three who go to the tomb only to find Christ risen. Lenina, of course, is appalled by the sight of blood, and then she and Bernard are addressed by the Savage – later called John – in the archaic Elizabethan English which is his bequest from Shakespeare. He, it seems, wished to be the one who was sacrificed; romantically, perhaps predictably, he falls in love with Lenina at first sight.

Again Huxley employs the structural device of retrospect as John tells the story of himself and Linda, but the narrative temperature is raised by Bernard's realization that Linda is the girl lost by the Director twenty-five years previously. Bernard's forward-looking mind now concentrates on the main chance, namely of frustrating the Director's attempts to have him sent to Iceland. Linda is now fat, coarse, dirty, obnoxious to Lenina, whom she envies so much ('those adorable viscose velveteen shorts'); she longs to return to the world of *soma* and to the standards set by the conditioning of her infancy ('Civilization is Sterilization'). Linda's is a brief but emotional account of her life in the Reservation and the birth of John, and then follows John's account of his own 'conditioning' and upbringing in the Reservation, the longest retrospective narration so far in the novel. The contrast with the treatment of the embryos in the brave new world will be readily appreciated; the story is largely direct from his consciousness *at the time* and so is imbued with the personal emotionalism so conspicuously lacking in the picture of society we have been shown in the era of Fordian stability. Prominent in this narrative are the child's reactions, Linda's physical suffering at the hands of the Indian women because of her 'promiscuity' with their men, John's own suffering at the hands of his 'mother' as she tries to deny her motherhood in line with her early conditioning; but within this narrative there is a further delving of the past, with Linda telling John of 'the other place' with its emphasis on cleanliness. John is thus forced to compare his mother's instruction with the wisdom and knowledge of the old men in the *pueblo*, the world of chemicals which she has described to him with the growth of the seeds in the womb of woman and the womb of nature. In the structure of the novel the language of the imagination now ousts the language of the scientifically created 'other place', and it stems from John's discovery of *The Complete Works of William Shakespeare* and how the words he finds there are equated with the experiences of life – with his feelings, for example, of jealousy of Popé (Linda's lover). John tells of how he stabbed Popé, how he worked with Mitsima, the old Indian, how he was rejected from the ritual and reveals how lonely and unfriended he has felt – a state of mind with which Bernard can identify sympathetically. We will recall, so tight is Huxley's sense of structure, that Helmholtz, too, is to explore loneliness, and we note further, in John's statement that he spent five nights on a mountain, a deliberate parallel with Christ in the wilderness. John of course identifies himself here and later with the Crucifixion and, when Bernard asks him if he would like to go to London, insists on having Linda go too, and expresses, in the words of Miranda in *The Tempest*, his rapture at the thought of seeing 'the other place' and of being with Lenina. Here the irony of the structure is deepened, since Miranda's own words in the play are an illusion, John's are an illusion soon to be punctured, and the whole of the Fordian world has its being in the illusion of *soma*.

Lenina, after 'the day of queerness and horror', takes sufficient *soma* to ensure a holiday, while Bernard – full of self importance – arranges with Mustapha Mond to bring Linda and John back with him. John is tempted by the sleeping Lenina, but rejects his own lust.

The first two sections of the novel are quite clearly defined, the initial focus being on the way of life – perhaps synthetic life would be more accurate – in the new world, while the second deals with the life and experiences of an individual in the Savage Reservation; the third section marks the return to the Fordian world, ending with the tragedy of John, his inability to face civilization which has sterilized human nature and replaced the right to choose for oneself by the compulsion of *soma*. The first step in the direction from which there is no return is taken with the public humiliation of the Director by Bernard; the poor man is called 'Tomakin' by the odious Linda and, worse, 'My father' by the moccasined John. Linda is put on ever-increasing doses of *soma* – no one wants to see her, she is too frightful – while John is courted by society as a freak who can be displayed for amusement, diversion, wonder. From now on the novel hastens to its terrible and terrifying climax, as Bernard seeks to exploit his discovery (and patronage) of the Savage in return for social (and sexual) favours. He is much sought after as he conducts John on his tour of the brave new world, the world that science has made; but John is sickened, mentally and physically, by the machine age he witnesses. He refuses to take *soma*, doesn't understand what is meant by elementary relativity, and visits Eton where he sees pupils laughing at the screened projection of 'savages' in the act of repentance. Lenina takes him to the feelies, which disgust him; he continues to desire her, but 'ashamed of his desire' does not spend the night with her afterwards, much to her chagrin, a chagrin which can only be alleviated by three half-gram *soma* tablets.

The last phase of the novel sees John in revolt, much to the social embarrassment of Bernard, who has invited such distinguished guests as the Arch-Community-Songster to meet 'Mr Savage'; John is reading *Romeo and Juliet*, and the Arch-Community-Songster has to make do with Lenina, who is going against her conditioning and becoming obsessed with John. Bernard, deflated, seeks out Helmholtz, who has himself fallen foul of authority by some rhymes on loneliness; Helmholtz and John get on well together, much to the jealousy of Bernard, and John reads Shakespeare to them, though Helmholtz cannot accept some scenes. It is significant that before the arrival of John there is no violence in this society, but when Lenina, suitably fortified with *soma*, attempts to ravish him, he assaults her physically (by hard slapping) and verbally with volley upon volley of apt Shakespearian quotation to define her immorality. Event follows event in a narrative rush as John races to the Park Lane Hospital for the Dying in time to watch Linda die, her last words being to Popé and not to him. John creates a scene in front of the children who are being death-conditioned by being fed chocolate éclairs and, mocked by his own words ('O brave new world'), he interferes with the *soma* distribution to the staff of the hospital, again using Shakespeare as a vivid rhetorical aid. In the most physically dramatic scene of the novel, Helmholtz fights beside him while Bernard flaps about, but the police arrive to pump *soma* vapour into the air (an advance, one supposes, on tear gas), and the Voice of Good Feeling establishes order and harmony again from its Synthetic Music Box. Significantly, Helmholtz and John have remained firm and continue to do so when they are brought before Mustapha Mond, but Bernard again regresses and becomes abject, blaming the other two.

Mustapha Mond explains why the feelies exist instead of *Othello*, why stability must be maintained, and how 'You've got to choose between happiness and what people used to call high art. We've sacrificed the high art. We have the feelies and the scent organ instead'. Again, Huxley makes use of retrospect as Mond tells of the Cyprus experiment where 22,000 Alphas were put together, all but 3000 of them being killed, such was the nature of the strife among the élitest group. Mond makes it clear that science and art are dangerous – he means positive discovery and originality – and tells how he had to choose between being sent to an island or training (and conforming) to be a Controller. Bernard has to be *soma*-sedated at the mention of the word 'island', and Helmholtz chooses to go to the Falkland Islands. The Controller and John discuss religion, and then the essential differences between the Controller's world, where everything is conditioned, are set against John's unequivocal assertion of individuality – 'I'm claiming the right to be unhappy'. Mond insists on going 'on with the experiment' with John, and the latter purifies himself by swallowing mustard and water. From now on he is always referred to as 'the Savage' – an ironic underlining by the author of his essentially civilized (in the human sense) nature. The Savage finds the solitude he wants, purifies himself by scrounging and simulating crucifixion, makes himself a bow and arrows (after all, he is a savage), but is discovered, filmed, overwhelmed by sightseers and, after beating Lenina, succumbs to *soma* and the raptures of 'orgy-porgy'. His guilt is so great the next day that he hangs himself in the lighthouse. The ending is the most poignant of masterstrokes, the tragic climax of the novel; it represents the death of the individual in his fight for the freedom to be miserable, to be happy, to be loving, to be jealous – in short to feel, and to feel not as others feel, but in his own separateness of being. The plot is thus a warning, a warning to man to beware of the power of science which, used as a political, moral, spiritual agent, could produce the kind of uniformity which is death-in-life rather than living.

Style

Brave New World is written in a variety of styles, but two major facets of its presentation are recognizably modern. The technique of exploring the consciousness, particularly in the case of John, is not revolutionary, since it derives in fact from the psychological realism of 19th-century novelists like George Eliot and Hardy; but earlier in the 20th century James Joyce had exposed the consciousness of Molly Bloom in *Ulysses* in its uninterrupted, unpunctuated flow, and although Huxley does not do this in *Brave New World* he does reveal the consciousness of character, particularly in relation to the past. Thus John's recollections of life with Linda in the early days on the *pueblo* are registered through the feelings of the child that he was; this is an imaginative leap by the author and shows character in the process of development, for John's human conditioning is made as psychologically true by this means as the mechanical conditioning of the embryos in *Brave New World* is made scientifically true. The second major aspect of Huxley's style is the allusive quality of so much of the writing, a technique of reference and association which is part and parcel of T. S. Eliot's poem *The Waste Land* (1922), where literary, anthropological, biblical and artistic allusions all abound. The result is an expansion of the text, for the associations set up by such a width of reference form an imaginative extension – they enrich, corroborate, exemplify on various levels what the author is trying to say to the reader. This allusive quality is one of the hallmarks of *Brave New World;* the names of the characters, for example, derive variously from science, politics, philosophy or the arts and are therefore part of the omniscient irony which runs throughout the novel and which contributes so much to its tone.

Brave New World deals with the power of science to establish uniformity, to kill what is individually imaginative and to replace it with the narrow compartments of fact or simulated sensation. What more fitting, then, that the author most referred to in the course of its pages should be Shakespeare, so that the text is speckled with quotations from the plays which expose the varieties of emotion and reaction – *not* uniformity of feeling –

but jealousy, suffering, ecstasy, the raptures of young love, mur-
derous intent, the lure of ambition, the fall from the pinnacle of
power? By impregnating his own writing with this range of
association – human, moving, vital – Huxley is lending emphasis
to the nullity of the society in the brave new world, the fact that it
craves sensation without moral or spiritual commitment and
shuns pain, old age, death, independence of spirit, the laughter
that is close to tears. Thus the use of Shakespearian language,
with its high degree of human experience, is a deliberate and
ironic contrast to the high degree of civilization which is sterilization, the negation of the individual. The irony is deepened, of
course, by the fact that most of Shakespeare's sublime expressions are uttered by the man who is considered a savage by the
automata who pass for human beings in the Fordian way of life.
This irony, which is most fully seen in the title of the novel itself,
thus extends throughout the text, and it is reinforced by a clever
and running use of cliché – 'straight from the horse's mouth' –
together with the employment of mannered colloquialisms
typical of English society in 1932, for example, 'They were dear
boys ... Charming boys!' and 'Hullabaloo'. Throughout, too,
there is a sense of parody, a fine ear for contemporary 'pop'
songs like 'There ain't no Bottle in all the world like that dear
little Bottle of mine'; and here Huxley is using current slang ('to
be on the bottle', 'to hit the bottle', meaning 'to get drunk') to
indicate a more serious aberration than drunkenness, in other
words the whole process of conditioning which has *soma* as the
permanent intoxicant and refuge. Equally effective is the parody of hymn tunes to be found in the Solidarity Service which
Bernard attends on alternate Thursdays, or the constant recur-
rence to games (obstacle golf, for example) which is satirical of
the English obsession with sport and competition. Irony and
satire, the latter an indication of the follies of man seen humor-
ously but correctively, are both integral to the style of *Brave New
World*. The hymn parody mentioned earlier is part of the satirical presentation of 'religion', for the worship of *Brave New
World* is the worship of Ford – our Freud – and, of course, of
soma. Hence the emphasis on 'the loving-cup of strawberry ice-
cream *soma*' as it is passed from disciple to disciple, and the
Arch-Community-Songster of Canterbury is represented as the
most social, most sexual, of men, but certainly not the most
spiritual.

The satire inherent in the style embraces most aspects of human behaviour, however dehumanized, in *Brave New World*. The speech inflexions of the Director and of Henry Foster, for instance, reflect the complacency of status and authority, as much applicable to our society and Huxley's contemporaries as they are to the Fordian ethos. Huxley has a fine ear for speech rhythms and what they reveal of character; consider the halting, archaic speech of John, or Linda's outburst when she sees Tomakin again. There is always vigour and freshness in Huxley's writing, and this is apparent when we consider another aspect of the style – the incidence of scientific or specialist words which, of course, reflect the scientific, compartmentalized society which is being described. These are heavily used in the early sections of the novel, where there is a need to establish categorically the *facts* of the society concerned; the language is consonant with, definitive of, those facts. Mention has been made of the structure of the novel earlier, and the style reflects the contrast between the early and late sections of the book; it is a calculated exploration of the effects of using scientific language followed by imaginative language. The contrast is further extended if we look at the presentation of character – and, more particularly, the language of the characters concerned which exemplify their habits and way of life – the Director, Henry Foster and Lenina early on, and John, Helmholtz and Mustapha Mond in the later sections of the novel.

I have already referred in passing to the choice of names for the characters, and the student is here directed towards the chapter notes which explore them at some depth if they are felt to be significant. Perhaps one should mention Ford as an example. Henry Ford was one of the great initiators of the age of materialism through the development on a large scale of the motorcar; while Freud, which Huxley's Ford sometimes called himself, was the virtual father of psychoanalysis and the examination of the subconscious, particularly in dealing with sexual behaviour and dreams. The duality of the name alone indicates the quality of Huxley's imagination and one of the salient elements of his style, for the society of *Brave New World* is both materialistic and sexual. Its subconscious is taken care of by *soma* – itself inducing a dream state – which provides the release from all tension. There is a gallery of portraits whose surnames and Christian names (perhaps one should say Fordian names) reflect the width of Huxley's cultural, historical and contemporary interests. We have only to see names like Marx, Hoover, Lenina (from Lenin), Diesel and Rothschild to be aware of the fact that there is no safety from Huxley's probing, resilient mind. The ten thousand names used, one suspects, are derived from those whose ideological or materialistic or scientific achievements have left some mark on history.

The play of irony through association is further seen when we consider Huxley's use of nursery rhyme, proverbial sayings and ritual, all marked aspects of his style in *Brave New World*. Particularly telling is the use of nursery rhyme, that basic imaginative standby of the early unscientifically-conditioned years, with its Listen-with-Mother associations, its state of innocence which contrasts so forcibly with Huxley's adaptations of it here. It goes without saying that the basis of 'orgy-porgy' is 'Georgy Porgy' who kissed the girls and made them cry. The next two lines of the original are curiously significant, and indicate Huxley's capacity to make the telling alteration:

But when the boys came out to play
Georgy Porgy ran away

This Huxley has changed to:

Boys at one with girls at peace,
Orgy-Porgy gives release.

Thus the fear element of the original has been transformed into the sharing (everyone belongs to everyone else), while the change of the word 'orgy' carries its own moral comment for the 20th-century reader. Moreover, in a terrible sense, we have adults behaving like children, but whereas children play in innocence and have the freedom to unleash their feelings, the adults of the brave new world are so conditioned (as children) that no *individual* feeling can be released without recourse to *soma*. It is a recognized fact that proverbial sayings are a part of our inheritance, in fact they underline in some ways the nature of our traditions. What more natural, then, that proverbial sayings should be debased into slogans in order to establish a 'tradition' of stability, acting as propaganda, part of the conditioning of tomorrow's citizens who will accept them and repeat them, dutifully, unknowingly, as truths? Huxley was always aware of the power of propaganda; after all, he had seen the effects of it in Italy during the Mussolini régime (his home was forcibly searched on one occasion). But in addition to this, such is his own ear for jingles and their rhythms, that he is able to anticipate satirically some of the advertising innuendo which has become so much a part of 20th-century life. Lenina is adept at repeating the catch-phrases of conditioning ('When the individual feels, the community reels', 'Was and will, make me ill' and that masterstroke of uniformity, 'A gramme is better than a damn').

Still more positive irony is to be found in Huxley's description of the feelies and the scent-organ, where there are certain anticipations of the way this branch of entertainment has developed, for example in terms of stereophonic sound. But the point of the irony here is barbed. If we consider the plot of the feely which John and Lenina watch we realize just how insidious is the propaganda of entertainment, with its deliberate reversal of 20th-century morality. *Three Weeks in a Helicopter* (perhaps we should ignore the fact that it is a Negro who has to go to the Adult Reconditioning Centre) demonstrates that everyone belongs to everyone else and that promiscuity is stability, since the Beta-Plus blonde is enjoyed by all three Alphas (and, of course, enjoys them); additionally, the class structure of AF 632 is reinforced, since it is the élite who display their superiority. Perhaps even more fundamental to the irony is the implication that a loss of individuality is a loss of perspective in the complete sense, for the focus is on the tactile effects of the bearskin rug rather than on the nature of the love-making on it. Again Huxley is writing with his contemporaries fully in mind, for they would not be unmindful of this knock at the bestselling novelist Elinor Glyn who, in her novel *Three Weeks* (1907), has several love-scenes on a tiger-skin rug which caused the novel to be branded as immoral and shocking.

Huxley's irony is also seen to good effect in the choice of imagery he employs, imagery from nature which stresses through contrast the lack of appreciation of nature in the way of life he is describing. The effect is often sudden, arresting, as for instance when Henry Foster takes Lenina to Stoke Poges for a round of obstacle golf and we are told that the 'humming of the propeller shrilled from hornet to wasp, from wasp to mosquito', which is a wry way of saying that science, in its quest for perfection, has imitated nature. In a civilization which has no domesticity as such Huxley delights in using figurative language which reminds the reader of real nature and real food rather than the synthetic substitutes which have replaced them; thus he speaks of the light as 'lying along the polished tubes like butter'; of two 'shrimp-brown children', while the sunshine is 'like warm honey'. Superbly casual images are sprinkled throughout the text, often reminding us that Huxley was a poet; Lenina after massage is 'like a pearl illuminated from within', and on another occasion the visible atmosphere is described as being like 'the darkness of closed eyes on a summer's afternoon'. The overall effect of these images is to sharpen our own awareness of the richness of the imagination, of life seen, felt, experienced, as distinct from life which is conditioned, simulated, sensationalized by chemical addiction.

Huxley's style, as I said at the beginning of this section is various; it is flexible, as we see from the inclusion of Helmholtz's poem in the text, which carries the implication that poetry, not *soma*, is the true release, the release of the individual from the inhibitions which his conditioning is supposed to have silenced. Part of Huxley's style in *Brave New World* consists of a running innuendo that human nature will survive, at least in individuals, the onslaughts of science.

This is merely a general introduction to Huxley's modes of writing in *Brave New World*, and the interested student will explore some of the areas, find his own examples in evidence, and perhaps even be moved to disagree with some of my instances here. There are further aspects of style to be uncovered; one might consider, for example, the quality of the dialogue used by Huxley, the nature of his physical descriptions (of people and places), and perhaps take a closer look at the kind of humour present in descriptions of man set on a misguided and dangerous course. In the notes on the separate chapters the student will find constant reference to Huxley's style and its effects. But *Brave New World* is imbued with a quality which is emotional rather than coldly intellectual, so that while we are aware throughout the novel of the range of Huxley's knowledge and interests, we are never allowed to forget that he is essentially humanistic in his concern for mankind, that his devotion is to the heart rather than the head, and that consequently the death of John – now the Savage – symbolizes the death of free-thinking, free-feeling man. The style is therefore prophetic and symbolic, symbolic of the future direction which mankind was likely to take through a too-strict adherence to scientific, materialistic and certainly psychological exploitation. Some of the prophecies have come true, and we are now in many ways, the slaves of what science has produced – the car, the supersonic aircraft, the television and the mass media, as well as the drugs, whether antibiotic, addictive or ephemeral. It is one of the marks of a great writer that his work will stand the test of time, and one of the exciting things about reading *Brave New World* today is that it has done just that; its style is lucid, vibrant with knowledge and imagination, colloquial, intellectual, humane. It is of its own time and of our time too, and its realities are present today and will perhaps colour tomorrow.

Chapter summaries, critical commentary, textual notes and revision questions

(*Note:* the summaries of chapters here are necessarily brief, since the section on 'Plot, Themes and Structure' contains much detail on the form the narrative takes in *Brave New World*. The textual notes must be used as aids to the critical appreciation and evaluation of the text; consequently, difficult words used simply and straightforwardly, and which can be looked up in a dictionary, are not usually listed here, and scientific terms of a specialized nature, i.e. which are not strictly speaking part of the *literary* content of the text, are also omitted.)

Chapter 1

The year is AF 632, AF standing for After Ford, and the Director of the Central London Hatchery and Conditioning Centre is conducting students around his establishment and pointing out to them the ways in which, from the embryo onwards, the human being is conditioned for a certain role in society; certain responses and functions are built in during this process. The means whereby up to 96 identical twins can be produced is mentioned and examined, this emphasis towards standardization being vital to the stability of the community. The whole scientific process of 'predestinating' the embryo is defined by Henry Foster, so that each individual belongs to one social and intellectual caste somewhere between the five grades of Alpha and Epsilon, with appropriate and matching physical attributes. Intelligence can be controlled, just as physique can be determined by, for example, reducing the amount of oxygen supplied to the embryo. As the Director puts it, 'All conditioning aims at . . . making people like their unescapable social destiny.' In passing we meet Lenina Crowne, who has a 'date' with Henry Foster, and then the group of students move off to the Decanting Room.

only thirty-four storeys A typical dry Huxleyan ironic aside which might almost go unnoticed. Doubtless it was a glance at the way society was developing its building in his own time – witness the skyscrapers of

New York and, today, our own tower blocks.

COMMUNITY, IDENTITY, STABILITY A deliberate and ironic contrast with what came to be the political creed of the French Revolution – Liberty, Equality, Fraternity.

a pale corpse-coloured rubber The image itself underlines the death-in-life existence which is going to be described, for 'conditioning' is moral death. The images in this paragraph are all of cold and death, thus stressing the absence of human warmth in a society which kills individuality.

lying along the polished tubes like butter an image carrying a reminiscence of domestic life – bread and butter – a life unknown to the inhabitants of the Fordian world.

Straight from the horse's mouth From one who knows, but the irony is in the use of this proverbial saying, which has here survived, although the traditions of life which made it have been supplanted by the scientific age.

For particulars, as everyone knows . . . generalities are intellectually evils To know a subject well and to keep to your allotted place in society makes for contentment, but understanding the broader principles is only necessary for the theorists.

fret-sawyers and stamp-collectors This reinforces the idea of the statement mentioned above, for both these are specialists in their way. 'Fret-work' was a very popular form of do-it-yourself furniture adornment in the twenties and thirties of this century.

incubators Apparatus for hatching, generally birds, but in this case, children.

gametes i.e. sexual protoplasmic bodies which unite with others for reproduction.

thermogene That which produces heat, especially in the human body.

salinity containing salts of alkaline metals or magnesium.

viscosity stickiness.

porous receptacle A container which allows the entry or exit of air or liquid.

bouillon Clear soup, a quietly ironic touch from the author in view of what he is describing.

Alphas . . . Betas . . . Gammas, Deltas and Epsilons The first five letters of the Greek alphabet, commonly used as a means of grading performance, for example, in assessing work in examinations. Here it is a subtly ironic reference to the Greek way of life, where society was as strongly class-structured as it is in *Brave New World* in terms of intellectual ability, right down to menial occupation.

Bokanovsky's Process It is clear what this means in the text, but the name, as with so many of Huxley's, is difficult to trace in the *real* as distinct from the *brave new* world. Maurice Bokanowski (1879–1928) was a French politician.

proliferate reproduce themselves, grow by budding.

burgeoned Put forth shoots, budded.

piddling Working or acting in a trifling way.

Podsnap's Technique Mr Podsnap is a character in Dickens's *Our Mutual Friend* (1864–5) who cleared away all difficult problems by saying, for example, 'I don't want to know about it. I don't choose to discuss it.' Huxley's reference is therefore finely ironic.

Singapore Island and about 50 islets off the Southern extremity of the Malay Peninsula. Important port, airport, trading centre, close to the equator.

Mombasa At the time of writing, capital of British East Africa.

pituitary i.e. an extract from the gland which is supposed to influence growth.

(but the light of combat . . . his chin was challenging) A superbly ironic addition by the author to indicate ambition and complacency at the same time.

decanted poured from a container.

peritoneum Double membrane lining the cavity of the abdomen.

morula A spherical mass of cells resulting from the cleavage of an ovum.

like the darkness of closed eyes on a summer's afternoon A fine natural image (remember the considerable trouble Huxley had with his own sight) which contrasts effectively with the artificial processes being described.

lupus Ulcerous disease of the skin.

Like chickens drinking Again an ironic comparison with what is natural, but there is stress too on the automatic, reflex action of the students, their lack of any individual response to what they are being told.

demijohns Bulging, narrow-necked bottles holding anything from 3 to 10 gallons.

Social Predestination Room This is where the embryos will be 'conditioned' for their future roles in life as Alphas, Betas etc.

blood-surrogate Substitute for real blood.

placentin . . . thyroxin . . . corpus luteum i.e. extracts and substances which are used to feed the embryo. There is a certain humour in Huxley which makes him use a group of scientific terms together, rather as Shakespeare in *Macbeth* has a witches' brew of unpleasant items from nature.

centrifugal Flying, tending to fly from the centre.

synthetic lung i.e. an artificially-produced lung.

'trauma of decanting' i.e. the emotional shock (to the embryo) of the process.

Foetal foal's liver The liver from an embryo foal, the offspring of a mare.

freemartins Imperfect females, in this case, sterile.

'mere slavish imitation of nature into the much more interesting world of human invention' A statement which underlines the basic theory that man, by rejecting nature, has made his own world an 'invented' one.

ingenuous Innocent, artless.

Ass! Again this is a form of irony, in that the Director is using upper-
class slang of Huxley's own time.

maturation Ripening, development.

abnormal endocrine coordination . . . postulated a germinal mutation
Unusual balance in the secretions of the endocrine gland . . . suggested
a change in the early stages of development.

Pilkington Really this process is one for making polished glass plate,
and is also, interestingly enough, known as the 'twin-plate' process,
hence its ironic use here by Huxley.

acetate-silk i.e. artificial, man-made.

**that is the secret of happiness and virtue . . . making people like their
unescapable social destiny** This is one of the first principles in the
Fordian philosophy, that conditioning prepares people for their role
in life and because of this preparation they are happy in it – they know
nothing else.

topsy-turvydom The explanation of this is simple – upside down – but
the irony is the author's own, since all morality is upside down in the
brave new world.

foetuses Embryos developed to a stage where their parts are
recognizable.

Chapter 2

The students proceed to the Neo-Pavlovian Conditioning
Rooms, the infant nurseries. Here the children instinctively
move towards what they see and therefore want, but alarm bells
followed by electric shocks ensure that they will learn to reject
the flowers and books which are put before them. This is the
basic means of conditioning, reinforced by hypnopaedia or
sleep-teaching, the discovery of which is recounted to the
students by the D.H.C. The students avidly note this historical
fact, and then witness a sleep-lesson on what is called 'Elementary Class Consciousness', or what the D.H.C. calls 'moral
education'. This is insidious propaganda, conditioning by repetition until it becomes part of the subconscious and then of the
conscious mind.

Neo-Pavlovian Modern or new, the techniques derived from those of
Ivan Pavlov (1849–1936), Russian physiologist, most famous for his
study of conditioned or acquired reflexes. He was awarded the Nobel
Prize in 1904.

viscose-linen Chemically-treated cellulose drawn into a yarn and,
presumably, combined with linen.

aseptically Surgically sterile, sterilized.

Aryan Indo-European, precursors of the modern European races.

nursery quartos Large printed books of rhymes and stories.

dumb-waiters Uprights with shelves which revolve, thus making the service (of food) easy.

pussy and cock-a-doodle-doo and baa-baa black sheep Note that what the children instinctively like is killed for them, thus indicating the anti-natural practices of the Fordian way of life.

What man has joined, nature is powerful to put asunder The meaning is obvious, but the irony is subtle, for there is an echo of the marriage service ('Those whom God hath joined together, let no man put asunder') – and the word 'wedded' has been used in the preceding line.

It was decided to abolish the love of nature . . . but not the tendency to consume transport Liking nature for itself is what is abolished, but setting sports, for example, in the country, will ensure that people travel to participate in them or to see them. It is the fundamental principle of Fordian economics – people must 'consume'.

Our Ford Here the echo of 'Our Lord' is specifically a reference to Henry Ford (1863–1947), motor-car manufacturer and therefore perhaps inadvertently the founder of the great materialistic age in which we live.

smut and pure science Smut means 'dirty talk', but parenthood is a scientific and human fact.

viviparous i.e. bringing forth young alive.

George Bernard Shaw . . . his own genius Shaw, often referred to as G.B.S. (1856–1950), playwright, essayist, social critic, philosopher, vegetarian; he was not slow to proclaim his own worth to a world which stopped its ears for some years, though he reached a wide audience with the publication of *St Joan* after the First World War.

first T-model This is a reference to the mass-produced cars from the Ford factories, 15 million in fact by 1928.

sibilant with the categorical imperative Notice how the silence is cleverly emphasized by the sound of the first word.

Elementary Class Consciousness i.e. taught about the different levels of society and their own place in it; but Huxley is also being satirical about the class-differences in his own society too.

asafoetida a resinous gum with a strong smell of garlic.

'The greatest moralizing and socializing force of all time' The words and the tone are the Director's, the irony Huxley's. 'Moralizing and socializing' can only mean 'conditioning' in any context in *Brave New World*.

Not so much like drops of water . . . one scarlet blob Two images, one from nature, one man-made, which emphasize the long-term effects of sleep-teaching.

Chapter 3

The D.H.C. and the students now watch the children at sexual play – part of their conditioning at this stage is the discovery of one another, as a prelude to sharing with everybody. Anyone who deviates from the normal range of erotic play – for example, not participating – is sent to see the Assistant Superintendent of Psychology. The D.H.C. gives an account of what things were like years ago before this enlightened age, but is interrupted by the arrival of Mustapha Mond, the Resident Controller for Western Europe. From now on there are alternations between Mustapha Mond's account of history (or the family unit of the past) with interpolations which involve Lenina and Bernard Marx. For instance, when Lenina arrives in the Girls' Dressing Room, the contrast is with the scents, perfume, massage, all the paraphernalia of hygiene which she enjoys, and the 'reeking with emotion' family life which is being narrated by Mustapha Mond. Thus, too, the monogamy of the past is deliberately compared with the 'everyone belongs to everyone else' which is the normal order of sexual behaviour in this Fordian day and age. Lenina is criticized by Fanny Crowne because she has been going out with Henry Foster – and no one else – for four months, a reversal of conventional morality, while Bernard (Mond's own commentary continuing all the time) is disgusted by Foster's and the Assistant Predestinator's discussion of Lenina. Lenina reveals to Fanny that she would like to 'have' Bernard, and that he had invited her to go to a Savage Reservation with him. Mustapha Mond continues to describe all the events which made their present way of life possible, complete with hypnopaedic slogans which are part of that present life – phrases like 'Ending is better than mending' and 'The more stitches, the less riches'. Lenina dresses for her 'date' with Henry Foster, Bernard is baited (mocked) by Foster and the Assistant Predestinator, and Mustapha Mond lectures on how old age was conquered by chemicals.

two nightingales soliloquized in the boskage They sang regardless of hearers in the wood. The nightingale is traditionally associated with poetry, but not here, since the only poetry in this society is written to conditioning order.

Centrifugal Bumble-puppy The game is described, but the important thing is to note how early the conditioning for adult games begins.

all the focused attention of scientists intent on a labour of discovery
Heavily ironic, since the children's discovery has to do with self, and the
implication is that the scientists are also motivated by self-interest.

Polly Trotsky Another fascinating Huxleyan choice of name. Trotsky
was a Russian revolutionary (1879–1940), who organized the revolt of
1917 with Lenin, fell out of favour with Stalin, was expelled from Russia
in 1929, and was assassinated in Mexico City in 1940.

surreptitious auto-erotism Spontaneous sexual emotion arising
without external stimulus.

fordship, Mustapha Mond 'Fordship' is obviously derived from
'worship'. The combination here appears to be that of Mustapha Kemel
(1881–1938), Turkish politician whose skilful leadership after the
overthrow of the Sultan caused him to be made first President of the
Turkish Republic, which he began to westernize; and Ludwig Mond,
distinguished chemist (1839–1909), who was one of the founders of
what ultimately became Imperial Chemical Industries.

Discarnate Parted from the flesh, disembodied.

Bernard Marx Karl Marx (1818–83) was the German founder of
modern international Communism.

Lenina Crowne from Lenin (1870–1924), prime organizer of the
Russian Revolution of 1917, greatly revered in Soviet Russia.

shrimp-brown children Vivid image from nature to stress an ironic
attitude to what is man-made.

History is bunk A phrase attributed to the *real* Henry Ford.

Harappa A village in Pakistan, where excavations revealed the remains
of a large city.

Ur of the Chaldees Important city of early Mesopotamia, reputedly the
home of Abraham.

Thebes One of the most famous cities of ancient Greece, associated with
the names of Cadmus, Dionysius, Oedipus and Hercules.

Babylon Ancient city, capital of Babylonia, famous for its gigantic walls,
hanging gardens, and rich, materialistic way of life.

Cnossos (Sometimes spelt Knossos) The centre of the Minoan
civilization in Crete; the palace of Minos, dated from the 18th century BC.

Mycenae The capital of Agamemnon's kingdom in the NE
Peleponnesus, site of many excavations yielding information about the
Ancient World.

Odysseus or Ulysses, subject of the epic poem by Homer which narrates
the ten years' wanderings of the hero after the fall of Troy and the
return to his native kingdom of Ithaca.

Job Biblical patriarch, noted for his wisdom and his suffering. For close
reference, see the Old Testament Book of Job.

Jupiter or Zeus, chief God of the Greeks, ruler of the world, father of
Gods and men, called by the Romans 'Jupiter', which means 'father of
the day'.

Gotama Sometimes spelled Gautama, chief deity of the Burmese, Buddha.

Athens The chief city of ancient Greece, the resort of able and wise men, particularly in literature and the arts, with monuments (of statue and temple, for example) reflecting its culture.

Rome Capital of modern Italy, founded by Romulus in 753 BC, with an unsettled history in pagan and Christian times.

Jerusalem Capital of Palestine, holy city of the Jews, frequently besieged, captured, destroyed, rebuilt.

the Middle Kingdom China.

King Lear Major tragedy by Shakespeare (1564–1616). The reference here is poignant and has echoes in the text, for in part Shakespeare's concern is old age, which has been abolished in the brave new world.

Thoughts of Pascal Blaise Pascal (1623–62). French writer and thinker. His *Pensées* were published after his death.

Passion Here, perhaps, a musical setting of Christ's sufferings on the cross.

Requiem A dirge, a musical setting for the repose of the souls of the dead.

Symphony A musical composition for full orchestra.

feelies i.e. so called colloquially throughout the novel because one can actually 'feel', experience, what is shown on the screen.

There's a love-scene on a bearskin rug ... For the nature of Huxley's irony here, see the chapter on 'Style' p.25.

periodically teeming women From time to time, giving birth to children.

chypre a perfume.

Psychically of the soul of mind.

midden dunghill.

like a pearl illuminated from within A typical imaginative Huxley coinage from nature to contrast with the synthetic life he is describing.

Pregnancy Substitute Since they do not have children themselves, drugs have to be administered to offset the psychological effects caused by not giving birth.

Intravenally into the vein or veins.

Our Freud Sigmund Freud, Austrian psychologist born in 1856, founder of the study of psychoanalysis and particularly concerned with the subconscious and the influence of family life on sexual behaviour. This reference is again evidence of Huxley's ironic skill in linking the great materialist (Ford) with the great analyst (Freud).

Samoa group of volcanic islands in the West Pacific.

New Guinea Island first colonized by the British and the Dutch.

like warm honey Again an image from nature to underline the author's criticism of the synthetic society.

Trobriands Group of islands in the Solomon Sea, the people being mainly Polynesian.

Musical Bridge Bridge is a card game resembling whist, and is widely played in England and America. The idea of a musical version is, of course, satirical.

monogamy The practice or circumstance of being married to one person at a time.

'But everyone belongs to everyone else' ... 'hypnopaedic proverb' One of the key proverbs of this society. The irony lies in the fact that it is 'sleep-taught', not arising naturally as a result of tradition or folklore.

axiomatic Truth based on established principle. Huxley follows it with 'self-evident', which admirably defines it.

as though to an invisible listener behind Lenina's left shoulder This casual statement contains a menacing overtone, for one gets the impression that anything unconventional will be reported to the authorities and punishment will follow. Helmholtz Watson and Bernard suffer in this way.

Mother, monogamy, romance ... how could they be stable? The whole paragraph should be studied carefully, for the inhabitants of *Brave New World* are conditioned against feeling, suffering, old age, temptation, everything that the Controller lists as disgusting in family life. The irony lies in the fact that John is later to claim the right to suffer, and to suffer in isolation if he so chooses.

He patted me on the behind ... the strictest conventionality This is the reversal of conventionality by our standard, but in *Brave New World* the standards are 'topsy-turvy'.

The machine turns ... have starved to death This paragraph stresses the economic nightmare of the industrial mechanized age. Presumably – it is here being retailed by the Controller as history – that stopping of the great industries meant starvation for millions before a new society, geared only to consumption and with each individual conditioned for his particular role, could be born.

'one's got to play the game' Again the use – ironically – of contemporary slang to indicate the reversal of standards in *Brave New World*.

Impulse arrested spills over ... those old unnecessary barriers This highly significant paragraph defines the scientific practice in that area of conditioning which changes or deflects the natural emotions into the disciplined and chosen outlets necessary for a stable society of stable individuals. It represents the killing-off of the individual response.

'Ford's in his flivver ... All's well with the world' A 'flivver' is a cheap motor car, the prototype Ford, but the irony is in Huxley's parody of Browning's *Pippa Passes* (1841): 'God's in His Heaven/All's right with the World.'

pneumatic Strictly speaking, it means acting by means of wind or air, but it is the epithet most used to describe sexual attractiveness in women in *Brave New World*. Presumably it means squeezable, rounded, voluptuous. Huxley is perhaps indebted to T. S. Eliot's *Whispers of Immortality*:

Grishkin is nice; her Russian eye
Is underlined for emphasis;

Uncorseted, her friendly bust,
Gives promise of pneumatic bliss.

Savage Reservation A tract of land for exclusive occupation by native tribes.

Obstacle golf Again Huxley is being ironic about the English obsession with games. Forms of obstacle golf are quite commonly found at seaside resorts today – and notice how the word 'obstacle' is used by the Controller in the next paragraph with an emotional emphasis.

Ectogenesis Development outside the body.

Pfitzner There was a German musician of this name (1869–1949), a romantic who went his own way and tended to ignore passing fashions.

liberalism i.e. favourable to democratic reforms and the abolition of privilege.

a round peg in a square hole Again the use of the proverbial, this time reversed, perhaps to emphasize the anti-human nature of what the Controller is saying.

physico-chemically equal The implication here is that in the composition of their bodily make-up they are equal, but that mentally they are not.

Phosgene ... Chloropicrin ... hydrocyanic acid A list of poison gases and poisons, presumably used in the Nine Years' war referred to by the Controller, and which helped to produce the reduction in the population needed before the Fordian era could be successfully established.

Kurfurstendamm A street in Berlin.

Eighth Arrondissement An administrative subdivision of a French department.

anthrax bombs These would be bombs which cause fatal malignant infection in man.

mucus Exuded shiny substance.

Ending is better than mending A basic piece of hypnopaedic teaching which ensures consumption and therefore the constant manufacture of goods.

The more stitches ... the less riches A complete turning about of the proverb 'a stitch in time saves nine'.

Simple Lifers i.e. those who believed in leading a life close to nature, without consuming goods. They are, of course, eliminated.

British Museum Massacre The British Museum, incorporating the British Library, is in Great Russell Street, Bloomsbury. It was founded as far back as 1700, but not opened until 1759.

And round her waist ... the regulation supply of contraceptives Superbly ironic description, a parody of the classical, somewhat mannered description of heroines – for example, Cleopatra – with Huxley assuming a deliberately mock-heroic poetic tone to indicate the unpoetic practicality of Lenina's apparel.

Malthusian Belt From Thomas Malthus (1766–1834), famous for his

Essay on the Principle of Population. He advocated moral restraint as a means of checking the increase of population.

the suppression of all books published before AF 150 i.e. because they would contain material from the unconditioned past which might inflame reactions and emotions. John, of course, discovers a prohibited book – Shakespeare – and lives by it.

bandolier A shoulder belt with cartridge loops.

fixation (of nitrogen) The process of combining a gas with a solid.

All crosses had their tops cut and became T's Obviously in worship of the T-model, the symbol of mass production.

morocco-surrogate Substitute leather.

Ford's Day Celebrations and Community Sings, and Solidarity Services Any state or ruling group establishes its own rituals, and the equivalents in our own society can be worked out. The rituals listed above have replaced religion, or rather, have become a religion of their own.

morphia and cocaine The first a narcotic used to alleviate pain, the second a drug producing insensibility.

were subsidized in AF 178 i.e. given grants so that they could work to produce *soma* for the world state.

'Euphoric, narcotic, pleasantly hallucinant' Producing happiness, inducing sleep, promoting pleasant illusions.

soma The drug having pleasant physical, mental, emotional effects. In reality, an intoxicating drink holding a prominent place in Vedic (Hindu) ritual. Its basis is the juice of the soma plant.

One cubic centimetre . . . ten gloomy sentiments Again the deliberately ironic use of the proverbial phrase, linked this time to the *soma* tablet.

Gonadal hormones Secretions to eliminate the physical effects of old age.

a gramme is better than a damn A proverb which establishes balance and conformity – no extremes of emotion.

physiological stigmata Definite characteristics of living functions.

such a crevice of time should yawn . . . magnetic Golf course to . . . Eight lines which define the conquering of old age, so that the old remain physically young; they will have no time to think, and in any case only need *soma* to cushion them against loneliness. The image 'crevice of time' is a fine way of indicating the possibility of 'slipping back' unless you have *soma*.

Revision questions on Chapters 1–3

1 Write an essay explaining in some detail the process of conditioning and its effects.

2 Write brief character-sketches from what you have learned so

far of (a) The D.H.C.; (b) Henry Foster; (c) Mustapha Mond.

3 Write an account of the history of the brave new world as far as you can piece it together from Mustapha Mond's and the D.H.C.'s statements.

4 Examine closely the techniques used by Huxley in Chapter 3, and say what effect they have on your appreciation of the novel so far.

5 Indicate, briefly, the nature of Huxley's style in these chapters.

Chapter 4

Lenina makes a point of engaging Bernard publicly in conversation about 'our New Mexico plan', and when she leaves him Bernard is confronted by the good-natured Benito Hoover, whom he hurriedly leaves. Meanwhile Henry Foster meets Lenina and they fly off in his helicopter to Stoke Poges to play a round or two of obstacle golf. Bernard broods on Lenina's conventionality, and then takes his own helicopter in order to pay a visit to Helmholtz Watson at the College of Emotional Engineering. Helmholtz is described in some detail; he is an Alpha-Plus, but has begun to be dissatisfied with his own existence and to question it, even to the extent of cutting his committees and his girls – and to cultivate being alone. He is somewhat disgusted by Bernard's abject self-pity.

dear boys . . . Charming boys The use of contemporary language again, indicating that Huxley's satire is of his own society as well as that of the future.

parathyroid i.e. the drug injected into the embryos from the thyroid gland.

Benito Hoover Curious, and typically Huxleyan linking, Benito being the first name of the Italian dictator Mussolini (1883–1945), while Hoover was the surname of the President of the United States elected in 1928.

Charing T-Tower Natural conversion of Charing Cross, London railway station.

simian ape-like, monkey-like.

was like a caress on the soft air Sensitive and imaginative conveying of atmosphere.

sex-hormone chewing-gum . . . plug . . . ruminating The satirical note is again obvious, with the idea that chewing-gum – widely used in America at the time of writing (1931) – should produce increased virility, but there is an association with nature through cows chewing the cud.

from hornet to wasp Here again man's imitation of what is natural is being stressed.

geometrical mushrooms A deliberately ironic linking of nature and mathematics.

Like the vague torsos of fabulous athletes . . . The affectation of a deliberately mock-heroic style, as inflated as the description itself.

The green was maggoty . . . Escalator Fives Courts 'Maggots' are a much-used term in the novel to describe the moral disease of society, and John uses it frequently during his clash with the children at the Park Lane Hospital for the Dying. These five lines indicate the 'consumption' of games. Since an escalator is a moving staircase, the idea of fives – a fast game played with bat or hand in a court with two, three or four walls – is humorous and ridiculous at the same time.

seven and a half hectares About 750 acres.

revitrifying converting into a glass-like substance.

aphides minute insects.

monorail single line or single rail.

Stoke Poges Parish and village in Buckinghamshire, Stoke Poges being a golfing club house. The churchyard, in which he is buried, is the scene of Gray's famous *Elegy* (1751).

College of Emotional Engineering The name is paradoxical, combining as it does, human nature and science, but there is an ominous overtone that emotion can be controlled, produced, put to practical and mechanical effect.

The Hourly Radio A touch of prophetic insight. 'News every hour, on the hour' is what we have today.

Gamma Gazette . . . Delta Mirror The first is suitable for middle-caste readers, while the second may be largely a picture paper, perhaps having associations with today's *Daily Mirror*.

their delicate work Heavily ironic.

Helmholtz Watson Herman von Helmholtz (1821–94) was an eminent German physiologist who did some original work on acoustics as related to optics, one particular work concentrating on the physiological basis for the theory of music, something which would have greatly interested Huxley.

feely scenarios i.e. written scenes for the films – the feelies are accompanied by a number of effects, as we learn when Lenina takes John to see *Three Weeks in a Helicopter*. (Remember that Elinor Glyn's novel which had the 'shocking' love scenes was called *Three Weeks*.)

Exmoor Wild tract of moorland in Devon, particularly famous for its ponies.

hullabaloo uproar – again a colloquialism.

the voluntary blindness . . . the artificial impotence of asceticism The highly intelligent could deliberately choose to test themselves in loneliness, and to be so severely abstinent or self-disciplined as to deny themselves their customary experiences.

Chapter 5

Henry and Lenina return from Stoke Poges. On their way back they watch the process of phosphorous reclamation from the dead, a subject which leads Henry to give a little social lecture. Then they make for the Westminster Abbey cabaret, where they dance the conditioned dance to 'Bottle of Mine' and then go back – 'bottled' – to Henry's apartment, *soma*- and contra-ceptively-prepared for the night. Bernard attends the Solidarity Service, which is held on alternate Thursdays, and has an acute sense of his own separateness from the others. The service is somewhere between a séance and a revivalist meeting in terms of the emotions generated, and ends in 'orgy-porgy', the 'liturgical' refrain which brings release, the ultimate in sexual self-indulgence. Bernard takes part, but he is not really part of it, and he experiences none of the ecstasy of the others.

Internal and External Secretion Trust . . . the lowing of thousands of cattle In his *Elegy* referred to earlier, Gray wrote that 'the lowing herd winds slowly o'er the lea', but these cattle have secretions taken from them to provide injections and chemicals for the conditioning process.

Farnham Royal A parish and village near Windsor.

Burnham Beeches In Buckinghamshire, near Maidenhead, and containing part of an ancient forest.

ant-like pullulation of lower caste activity Here the budding and sprouting of mass uniformity is being stressed.

Slough Crematorium Slough is in Berkshire, 21 miles from London.

the soothing, the smoothing . . . Notice how the repetition, alliteration and rhyming perfectly convey the drowsiness of the mood.

Westminster Abbey Cabaret The centre for the nation's Christianity in the past has become, ironically, the centre for its leisure activity in AF 632.

CALVIN STOPES AND HIS SIXTEEN SEXOPHONISTS A superb, at first sight paradoxical, combination. John Calvin (1509–64), the Protestant reformer, and Dr Marie Stopes (1880–1958), suffragette, pioneer advocate of birth control. The saxophone, a keyed wind instrument, was very popular at the time when Huxley was writing.

ambergris and sandalwood The first a wax-like substance used in perfumery, the second scented wood.

There ain't no Bottle in all the world It reads like the parody of a popular song, and perhaps glances as well at the consumption of alcohol in contemporary society.

like melodious cats Hardly a flattering reference to the quality of the music.

deturgescence 'Turgescence' is morbidly inflamed or swollen, so this is the reverse.

diminuendo gradually decreased loudness of.

a bottled ocean of blood-surrogate ... Bottled they crossed the street Both these images stress that conditioning is a substitute for living, and that the people are so addicted that they have no independent life.

Aphroditeum so named after Aphrodite, Greek Goddess of Love, but with a glance at a prominent English club, the Athenaeum.

Carrara-surrogate Imitation marble.

Ludgate Hill Railway station in London. Ludgate Hill runs between St Paul's and Fleet Street.

Big Henry, the Singery Clock Obviously a reference to the Fordian equivalent of Big Ben, the famous bell in the clock tower of the Houses of Parliament. Remember that Ford's first name was Henry.

Morgana Rothschild The surname is from the family of famous German financiers who have exerted a tremendous influence on international banking; the name is synonymous with great wealth.

atonement making amends for, expiating.

Fifi Bradlaugh Charles Bradlaugh (1833–91) was a freethinker who refused to take the oath on entering Parliament in 1880. He was expelled and re-elected regularly, but allowed to take his seat finally in 1886 until his death.

Joanna Diesel Rudolph Diesel (1858–1913) German engineer, gave his name to the type of oil-engine in which ignition of fuel is produced by the heat of air suddenly compressed.

Clara Deterding Deterding was an Anglo-Flemish financier (1866–1939), a director of Shell, and a very important figure in the oil world.

Sarojini Engels Friedrich Engels (1820–95) was the founder of scientific socialism. He lived mostly in England, where he wrote *The Condition of the Working Classes in England* (1844).

Herbert Bakunin Mikhail Bakunin (1814–76) was a Russian anarchist, opposed to the ideology of Karl Marx.

the yearning bowels of compassion tender feelings, pity.

The dedicated soma tablets ... The loving-cup of strawberry ice-cream The parody is of church services and rituals.

I drink to my annihilation ... to being made one of the many, but not single or alone.

Ford we are twelve ... has but begun The 'shining flivver' is the symbol of the machine age, there is a strong emphasis on the social stability, and the idea is the renunciation of self and to become part of the great social entity.

Feel how the Greater Being comes ... For I am you and you are I A 'spiritual' extension of the fact that everyone belongs to everyone else.

the solar plexus the complex of nerves at the pit of the stomach.

**with a touch, released a delirium of cymbals and blown brass, a fever
of tom-tomming** Notice that the noise of the ritual which is stressed
here is equivalent to that of the Indians in the Savage Reservation,
thus underlining the fact that despite conditioning, human needs and
responses are the same.

it was as though she were having her throat cut The implication is
that, violence having been eliminated from *Brave New World*, the
simulated emotions induced by drugs are an approximation to reality
or real feelings.

each with hands on hips of the dancer preceding Huxley would not be
unmindful of dances like the conga which would be popular at the
time.

'Orgy-porgy' Here a clever parody of the nursery rhyme 'Georgy
Porgy pudding and pie,/Kissed the girls and made them cry'. As usual,
the Huxley version carries its own irony.

the liturgical refrain Strongly religious, a liturgy being a form of
public worship which, of course, this song and the Solidarity Service
exemplify.

Chapter 6

Lenina is faced with the decision as to whether or not she should
go to New Mexico with Bernard. She has been to the North Pole
previously, and found that a sufficiently chastening experience.
She goes out with Bernard only to discover that he would rather
walk and talk than play electro-magnetic golf. They fly to
Amsterdam and back (having watched part of the Women's
Heavyweight Wrestling Championship); Bernard tried hard to
explain his thoughts and emotions to Lenina; ultimately he gives
up and becomes a little hysterical, but goes to bed with Lenina
(after swallowing sufficient *soma*); the next day he is conscience-
stricken and considers that they have behaved like 'infants' by
not waiting. Next Bernard goes to the D.H.C. to get his permit
to go to Mexico signed, and listens, somewhat shocked, to the
D.H.C.'s story of his own visit there some 25 years previously
with a Beta-Minus who subsequently disappeared into the
mountains. The D.H.C.'s reaction to his own weakness in
revealing this to Bernard is to reprimand him and warn him
sharply about his unconventional conduct. Bernard, elated,
leaves, and then he sets off with Lenina, to whose delight they
spend a luxurious night at Santa Fé before going on to the
Reservation. Here the Warden gives them an account of the

conditions there, stressing that there is no escape. Later Bernard phones Helmholtz and learns – now to his dismay – that he (Bernard) is to be recommended for transfer to Iceland. He swallows four tablets of *soma* and they go on to Malpais.

Jean-Jacques Habibullah Jean-Jacques Rousseau (1712–78), French political philosopher and educationist. In view of the nature of Fordian society, Rousseau's most famous statement could be applied here: 'Man is born free, and everywhere he is in chains.'

Oxford Union The home of the University Debating Society, which often invites distinguished speakers to take part.

St Andrews In Fife, Scotland, the home of the Royal and Ancient Club (golf) founded in 1754.

Skiddaw Mountain in Cumberland, now Cumbria, 3000 feet high, near Keswick.

Semi-demi-finals presumably the equivalent of what are called the quarter-finals today.

A gramme in time saves nine A simple parody of 'A stitch in time saves nine', but it ominously underlines the possible extent of addiction.

When the individual feels the community reels i.e. because individuality, or the expression of it, would undermine stability.

genial Ford-speed The equivalent would of course be either 'God speed' or 'God be with you' or simply 'Good luck'.

solecism an error of taste.

Bottomless Past Presumably the equivalent of 'Go to Hell'.

Texas The second-largest state of the United States of America.

New Orleans Large city in Louisiana, USA.

Santa Fé The state capital of New Mexico.

Aurora Boa Palace The first two words refer to the phenomenon of the northern lights which radiate from the magnetic pole.

caffeine Vegetable alkaloid found in coffee and tea plants.

brachycephalic short-headed.

Grand Canyon A gorge in North Arizona 280 miles long, 4–18 miles wide, a famous national park and a natural monument.

totemism The worship of the North American Indians, emblems of clans or individuals.

Zuni The language and the valley of the Zunis in New Mexico.

Athapascan The language of a widely spread people in North America.

stoicism from the school of philosophy founded in Athens in 308 BC by Zeno, which taught developing control of the passions and indifference to pleasure and pain; it has come to mean self-control and fortitude.

'Was and will make me ill ... I can take a gramme and only am' Sleep-taught proverbs, again indicating the nature of *soma* addiction throughout society.

Five minutes later roots and fruit . . . rosily blossomed A fine use of imagery by Huxley, since the natural world is wiped out by the use of *soma*, but the language used to describe the feelings involved refers back *to* nature.

octoroon having one-eighth Negro blood.

pueblos Spanish American towns or villages, settlements of Indians.

Malpais Perhaps a play on the word 'unpleasant' in view of the way it affects Lenina.

mesa A high tableland.

A mosaic of white bones Finely poetic observation bearing in mind that real death – not the death of those in the brave new world – is involved.

fulminated as though by a poetic justice Exploded, detonated, which was what they deserved since they were predatory.

Taos and Tesuque . . . Ojo caliente The interested students can trace this journey by studying a map of New Mexico, where Taos, Nambe, Laguna and Acoma are all prominently marked. (See *Encyclopaedia Americana* Volume 20, pages 184–188b for map and some detail on the Indian Reservations.)

Chapter 7

Bernard and Lenina are conducted to the *pueblo* by a guide, who is revolting to Lenina because of his smell; they pass natives who are carrying snakes, and the combination causes Lenina to recoil; she is further disgusted by the dirt and dust at the entrance to the *pueblo*. Next she sees an old man – remember that old (physical) age has been eliminated in the brave new world – and then a woman giving suck to her baby; the reaction from Bernard is one of exaggerated praise for what he sees. Lenina has to suffer more horrors before they are taken to watch the ritual initiation of a young man, who is beaten until he bleeds before being left, and then taken into one of the houses by three women. Lenina's anguish is now acute, particularly as she has forgotten to bring her *soma* with her. But suddenly they are confronted by a young man, who addresses them in archaic, Elizabethan, English; he reveals that he would have liked to be the young man of the initiation ceremony. He tells them about himself and his mother, who is obviously, as it turns out, the girl who was left in the mountains some 25 years earlier by the D.H.C. Linda, for that is her name, has also suffered the advance of age and grossness, but she is delighted to see Lenina whose feelings of nausea outweigh everything else. Linda's account of her own life on the Reservation makes harrowing reading as we see how ill-prepared she was by her conditioning to face the realities of *feeling* and physical work.

like a ship becalmed in a strait of lion-coloured dust The still, arid colour effects are interesting, and the mention of 'lion' brings us – or rather Lenina and Bernard – face to face with nature.

stepped and amputated pyramids A superb image in terms of perspective – the Savage Reservation is old in time, like the pyramids – and unlike Fordian society.

the rhythm of that mysterious heart The primitive beat that appeals to instinct, but ironic since it has its equivalent in the Solidarity Service and, perhaps, in an emasculated way, in the music played by the Sexophonists.

like asphalt tennis-courts Lenina's choice of image is appropriate to her conditioning – the 'consumption' of what is man-made.

'cleanliness is next to fordliness' ... 'civilization is sterilization' The first is a straight adaptation of 'cleanliness is next to godliness', while the second conveys the irony of its origin, i.e. that too much civilization leads to the sterilization of individuality.

a mask of obsidian vitreous lava, or volcanic rock like bottle glass. The effect would certainly shock Lenina.

metabolism The building up of nutritive material into living matter.

ophthalmia inflammation of the eye.

goitre enlargement of the thyroid gland, with consequent swelling in the neck.

coyote the North American prairie-wolf.

'A most unhappy gentleman' The first of the many Shakespearian or Shakespeare-associated references from John. There are over 500 references to 'gentleman' in the *Shakespeare Concordance*, but I have not found this one.

'Do you see that damned spot?' A half quotation from *Macbeth* (Act V Scene i), the celebrated sleep-walking scene of Lady Macbeth.

'The multitudinous seas incarnadine' *Macbeth*, Act II Scene ii.

'They disliked me for my complexion' John sometimes quotes accurately, sometimes not. This should read: 'Mislike me not' (*Merchant of Venice*, Act II Scene i).

mescal This is made from the dried tops of the small cactus, and has narcotic and intoxicating properties.

peyotl This is a beverage made from a species of cactus in Mexico.

Streptocock-Gee to Banbury T Again the adaptation of the simple, innocent nursery rhyme to fit in with the civilized and sterilized society being described in *Brave New World*.

Revision questions on Chapters 4–7

1 Compare and contrast the characters of Bernard Marx and Helmholtz as they have been revealed so far.

2 Indicate the main targets for Huxley's irony and satire in these four chapters of the novel.

3 Show how Huxley makes use of the past, with particular reference to Chapter 7.

4 Write on the main aspects of Huxley's style which you find interesting in this section of the book.

5 Compare and contrast any aspect of life in the brave new world with that of the Indians in the Reservation.

Chapter 8

John gives Bernard an account of his life for as far back as he can remember. It is intimate, warm, dirty, with his jealousy of the men who come to see Linda, the description of the women beating Linda, and the latter's alternations between rejection and love in the motherhood she has been conditioned to despise. Linda tells him all about the 'other place', and John tells of his childhood with her and with the other children in the *pueblo*. He remembers how he learned to read, how the other boys mocked him and made up songs about Linda, and how he discovered the old, battered volume of *The Complete Works of William Shakespeare*. The words soon begin to mean something to him, just as the words, the lore and the legends of the Indians constitute his 'conditioning' at the same time. Equating the words with his own feelings – the words of Shakespeare, that is – he attacks Popé, and wonders to find himself spared by Linda's lover. Then he learned how to fashion pots in clay from Mitsima, but when the time comes for the boys' initiation into manhood he is rejected and, in his loneliness, goes away into the mountains and tries to experience the intense suffering of the crucifixion. When Bernard tells John that he will take him to London, John (after stipulating that Linda must come too) is so elated that he uses Miranda's words to express his wonder and excitement.

tortillas Flat maize cakes, the equivalent to the Mexican of bread.
Bye, Baby Banting A 'bantling' is a young child, so Huxley has here

adapted the word to make his version of the nursery rhyme easy on the tongue. The original of course would be from 'Bye, Baby Bunting,/Daddy's gone a-hunting'.

gourd The rind of a flesh fruit, which would have been emptied from it.

Transformer of the World, Right Hand and Left Hand ... Our Lady of Acoma These references appear to be mixed, some of the lore, legends, in fact the mythology of the Indians and some of the Christian influences which have coloured John's early life.

THE CAT IS ON THE MAT. THE TOT IS IN THE POT Basic reading jingles, subtly altered by Huxley, and contrasting vividly with the lore and legends of Indian life which form the other part of John's 'conditioning'.

'Nay but to live ... Over the nasty sty' *Hamlet*, Act III Scene iv. The words, unbeknown to John, give expression to his jealousy of Popé.

A man can smile and smile ... lecherous, kindless villain A running on of the jealousy sequence, seen here in Hamlet's denunciation of Claudius. The quotations are from *Hamlet:* the first from Act 1 Scene v, the second from Act II Scene ii.

'When he is drunk ... Or in the incestuous pleasures of his bed' *Hamlet*, Act III Scene iii.

'A, B, C, Vitamin D, The fat's in the liver, the cod's in the sea' Once more, the effective parody of the nursery-rhyme, with an immediate contrast in the succeeding line, where Mitsima sings of killing a bear. In *Brave New World* scientifically-evaluated food is the only important food.

Tomorrow and tomorrow and tomorrow ... Macbeth's famous soliloquy after the death of Lady Macbeth (Act V Scene v).

Miranda The heroine of *The Tempest*, brought up by her father on the 'enchanted isle', nearly ravished by Caliban, betrothed to Ferdinand, son of Alonso.

'O, wonder! How many goodly creatures are there here: How beauteous mankind is! ... O brave new world that has such people in it' *The Tempest*, Act V Scene i.

Chapter 9

Lenina's agonies have been such after her first day at Malpais that she takes a *soma* holiday. Bernard telephones Mustapha Mond to get permission to bring John and Linda back to London, and meanwhile John visits the sleeping Lenina, with whom he has fallen romantically in love at first sight. He is so moved by the sight of her that he speaks aloud the only language he knows which can suitably convey his feelings – the verse of *Romeo and Juliet*. He is tempted to 'unzip' Lenina but resists the temptation and emerges in time to see Bernard, whom he thought had gone for good, climb out of his helicopter.

Safe as helicopters Unobtrusively adapted from the saying, 'safe as houses', with the added irony that in the past it would have seemed risky to fly, but all things are made possible – and safe and sure, perhaps – by science.

filling his lungs with her essential being Again this is finely ironic, since what John is drinking in is the atmosphere – of perfume – and then he proceeds to examine her clothes. Lenina has no 'essential being'; she is as synthetic as the scent and clothes which help to make her attractive.

Her eyes, her hair, her cheek . . . The cygnet's down is harsh This is Troilus's lyrical description of Cressida in Act I Scene i of *Troilus and Cressida*.

On the white wonder of dear Juliet's hand, may seize . . . thinking their own kisses sin *Romeo and Juliet*, Act III Scene iii. Both this quotation and the one preceding it are romantic expressions of love which fit John's mood here.

Dare to profane with his unworthiest hand John is adapting Romeo's words in Act I Scene v to meet his own needs.

with the gesture of a dog shaking its ears as it emerges from the water This is a simple and effective image which shows just how close to nature John himself is. We remember how appalled Lenina was by the sight of a dog!

agaves Plants which include the American aloe among their numbers.

Chapter 10

Meanwhile, back in the Bloomsbury Centre, the D.H.C. is waiting to receive Bernard and to denounce him publicly prior to his transfer to Iceland. Bernard, secure in the knowledge that he holds the trump cards, produces them; the D.H.C. is appalled at the sight, the grotesque sentimentality of Linda, who approaches him, calling him 'Tomakin', while John simply greets him, with great humility, as 'My father'. To the students and workers in the centre it is a huge practical joke; to the D.H.C. it is indescribable anguish – and the end of his career.

recapitulated aeons immeasurable periods, here heavily ironic.

hunt-the-slipper a parlour game much played in the past, with one player in the middle having to guess who has the slipper as it is passed from one person to another. Here it looks to be a misprint for *hunt-the-zipper*, which is referred to elsewhere in *Brave New World*, and which would be far more suited to 'erotic play'.

'Unorthodoxy threatens more . . . it strikes at Society itself' This is the
basic creed of *Brave New World*. Helmholtz, Bernard and, ironically, in
the past, the Controller, are all guilty of unorthodoxy.

unfordly The equivalent of 'ungodly'.

undulation In view of Linda's size, there is a fine irony in this choice of
word, which means wavy, going alternately up and down.

'My father' Dirty words, the most socially damning which could be
uttered, and they thus presage the end of the Director's career.

obliquity A slanting or declining from the normal.

a scatological rather than a pornographic impropriety The distinction
is a fine one, but what it appears to mean is that the word 'father' is
literary filth rather than filthy action according to the standards of
Brave New World.

Chapter 11

General description of the reactions to the arrival of Linda and
John; the latter is much sought after, but Linda is put on a
permanent *soma* holiday which is intended to kill her off, though
John raises objections to it. In any case, society is not interested
in seeing something as physically repugnant as Linda; John is
the one they all want to see, and Bernard is able to take advantage of his new-found status to 'have' as many girls as he wants
and to enjoy a way of life of which he was so critical earlier.
Filled with elation, he conducts John about to show him the
sights and practices of this brave new world, and writes pompous reports to Mustapha Mond which afford the Controller
some amusement. But the physical uniformity produced by the
Bokanovsky process is too much for John, and he is made
physically sick as a result. The visit to Eton is even more repugnant to him, since he sees the *Penitentes* of Acoma prostrating
themselves and wailing, and finds that the reaction of the Eto-
nians is that they 'fairly shouted with laughter'; he also sees the
Synthetic Music Boxes for each dormitory, while a later visit to a
factory reveals that the workers are issued with a daily *soma*
ration. Lenina, also, has entered into a new social whirl because
of her connection with John; she finds herself becoming very
interested in him, and together they go to the feelies to see the
current 'hit' release, *Three Weeks in a Helicopter*. John's reaction,
to Lenina's amazement, is that the feely was 'base' and 'ignoble'.
And to her greater wonder, John does *not* spend the night with
her.

'**Eternity was in our lips and eyes,**' *Antony and Cleopatra*, Act I Scene iii.

patchouli tap Containing perfume obtained from an odoriferous Indian plant.

Dravidian twins Non-Aryan, coming from Southern India or Ceylon.

'**Ariel could put a girdle round the earth in forty minutes**' Puck could certainly do it (see *A Midsummer's Night's Dream*, Act II Scene ii), but perhaps John, being in love, has forgotten that Ariel's accomplishments were rather different.

prognathous having projecting jaws.

But the Savage . . . was violently retching . . . as though the solid earth had been a helicopter in an air pocket. A superb mixing of the natural and the new – uniformity produces sickness in one who might be expected to be sick with a new experience, i.e. flying in a helicopter.

Eton . . . School Yard . . . Lupton's Tower Eton was founded in 1440–1 by Henry VI. In School Yard, which is the nucleus of the school, there is a statue in bronze of the founder. The ensuing account in *Brave New World* indicates the changes wrought at Eton, among them the 'chrome-steel statue of our Ford'.

Miss Keate, the Headmistress John Keate was a reforming Headmaster of Eton 1809–34.

elementary relativity Einstein's theory of the universe, the principle that all motion is relative.

Penitentes of Acoma the worshippers, various Roman Catholic orders associated for mutual discipline.

Savoy A famous hotel in the West End of London.

those caskets? Whoever chooses the right casket will marry Portia. Many references are made to them in *The Merchant of Venice*, Acts I and II.

Young Women's Fordian Association This is the equivalent of the Young Women's Christian Association, which has many branches and ʾostels in Great Britain.

Arch-Community-Songster of Canterbury A fine, satiric equivalent to the Archbishop of Canterbury.

Deauville Fashionable resort in northern France, famous for its casino, beach, horse-racing and leisured, international society.

Hug me . . . Love's as good as some Huxley's ear for the 'pop' lyric is exemplified here, but the overtones, in view of *soma* addiction, are serious.

Herbal Capriccio a lively musical composition, the 'herbal' being ironic.

arpeggios striking of notes of chord in succession.

Mozart (1756–91) Born in Salzburg, eminent composer, particularly noted for his operas.

erogenous zones i.e. places on the body which respond most strongly to sexual stimulation.

Alhambra originally, the Palace of the Moorish Kings in Granada.

a cocked hat set aslant.

like a dying moth that quivers, quivers . . . Again the image from
nature, sounding the irony at sensations scientifically created.

fine shuddering roads of anxiety and pleasure across her skin Unusual
imagery, but it indicates the power of the sensations thus created.

base . . . ignoble The combination of these two words occurs twice in
Henry VI.

turned with religious care its stained and crumpled pages The effect
of this is immediate, almost as if John reveres what he finds in
Shakespeare as distinct from what he finds in life in the brave new
world.

Chapter 12

For Bernard's most important social evening – with the Arch-
Community-Songster of Canterbury present – John shuts himself away and refuses to come out. Lenina feels herself strongly
attracted to John ('Her heart seemed to stop beating'), while
Bernard experiences a loss of face which is made implicit by the
comments, both to him and behind his back, of the important
guests. Even the champagne-surrogate cannot lighten the atmosphere. John continues to read *Romeo and Juliet*, Mustapha Mond
censors an original paper called 'A New Theory of Biology',
Lenina goes off with the Arch-Community-Songster, Bernard
awakes next morning to a bad old world, and goes to see Helmholtz for sympathy; the latter has got himself into trouble with
the authorities by writing a poem which explores the feeling of
loneliness. Later he meets John, listens to his readings from
Shakespeare, and they get on extremely well together, much to
the jealousy of Bernard. Helmholtz has the grace to apologize to
John for laughing at a particular aspect of *Romeo and Juliet*.

carotene This provides the colour in butter and carrots, a precursor of
Vitamin A.

collation A light meal.

St Helena A volcanic island in the south-east Atlantic, the scene of
Napoleon's imprisonment from 1815 until his death in 1821.

'O she doth teach the torches . . . for earth too dear' *Romeo and Juliet*, Act
I Scene v. This epitomizes romantic love, which John worships, as
distinct from the temptations of the flesh.

**One of the principal functions of a friend . . . to inflict upon our
enemies** A piece of Huxleyan wisdom and psychological truth. It
means that because our friends are vulnerable we take advantage of
them.

Yesterday's committee . . . seem so squalidly Superbly economical poem with alternate lines rhyming, which explores the lack of anything in life, in which people and machines are compared and found to be the same basically, i.e. lacking essential being.

Egeria's Egeria was a nymph who was celebrated for framing forms of worship for the Roman community, and hence her name has become synonymous with that of 'spiritual adviser'. Obviously Helmholtz is using her name ironically.

Let the bird of loudest lay . . . Saw division grow together *The Phoenix and the Turtle*, mysterious and intense poem by Shakespeare, full of emotion and fantasy; its sudden departures and arresting, apparently unrelated images, obviously appeal to the mind of Helmholtz.

the shattering and defilement of a favourite poetic crystal A fine image to define the nature of John's and Helmholtz's sensitivity; it also diminishes Bernard's character.

That old fellow . . . Casual and colloquial reference to Shakespeare.

'Is there no pity . . . where Tybalt lies' *Romeo and Juliet*, Act III Scene v.

pearl from before swine This time rather a poignant adaptation of the proverb.

Chapter 13

Lenina, quite distracted by the thought of John, refuses to go out with Henry Foster, and forgets to give one of the embryos in her charge its sleeping-sickness injection. Fanny urges her to visit John and, suitably fortified with *soma*, she does. She does not understand the individuality of his reactions or his feelings, and her attempted seduction of him brings down on her head – and her body – both physical and verbal abuse, the latter culled almost exclusively from Shakespeare. Eventually she escapes by shutting herself in the bathroom; meanwhile John has a phone call to tell him that Linda is dying.

A doctor a day keeps the jim-jams away 'An apple a day keeps the doctor away' implies that nature provides a better cure than medicine, but in *Brave New World* nature has been abolished and the only cure is that supplied by science.

adage traditional maxim or proverb.

Mwanza-Mwanza Three places of this name are listed in *The Times World-Index Gazetteer*: in the Congo, in Malawi and in Tanganyika.

trypanosomiasis Sleeping-sickness caused by a blood-parasite.

'Admired Lenina . . . indeed the top of admiration . . . of every creature's best' Ferdinand's loving appraisal of Miranda (*The Tempest*, Act III Scene i).

'There be some sports are painful . . . some kinds of baseness are

nobly undergone' Some slight misquotation, but substantially from Ferdinand's speech in *The Tempest* (Act III Scene i).

An emblem of the inner tide of startled elation Huxley's words, but somewhat poetic, since they convey one of the few individual responses of which Lenina is capable.

'Outliving beauty's outward, with a mind that doth renew swifter than blood decays' *Troilus and Cressida*, Act III Scene ii.

'If thou doest break her virgin knot ... may with full and holy rite' Prospero's caution to Ferdinand (*The Tempest*, Act IV Scene i).

blackamoor a Negro, dark-skinned.

'The murkiest den ... mine honour into lust' Ferdinand's response to Prospero's caution (*The Tempest*, Act IV Scene i).

'For those milk paps ... Be more abstemious or else' The last part of this is from *The Tempest*, Act IV Scene i; the first part from *Timon of Athens*, Act IV Scene iii.

like a neatly-divided apple The image is from nature, the temptation strongly reminiscent of Eve.

'Whore! Impudent strumpet' *Othello*, Act IV Scene ii.

'The wren goes to't ... to sweeten my imagination' *King Lear*, Act IV Scene vi.

'O thou weed ... Heaven stops the nose at it' *Othello*, Act IV Scene ii.

'The devil Luxury with his fat rump and potato finger' *Troilus and Cressida*, Act V Scene ii.

'If I do not usurp myself, I am' *Twelfth Night*, Act I Scene v.

Revision questions on Chapters 8–13

1 What elements of humour do you find in Huxley's portrayal of John's reactions to the society of *Brave New World*?

2 How important are the references to Shakespeare in these sections of the novel? How are they related to Huxley's message?

3 What changes or developments do you note in the characters of Bernard Marx and Helmholtz Watson? You should refer closely to the text in your answer.

4 Write an appreciation of Huxley's use of nature in *Brave New World*.

5 Write an appreciation of Helmholtz's poem, saying how it is related to the theme of loneliness in the novel, with particular reference to John.

6 Compare and contrast John's reactions to Lenina and Lenina's reactions to John, using quotation where appropriate to support your views.

Chapter 14

John arrives at the Park Lane Hospital for the Dying and immediately makes his presence felt by the nature of his personal concern for his 'mother', something that the staff are not used to coping with. Linda is watching, in so far as her drugged state will allow her to, the inevitable television games, and although she recognizes John momentarily she soon reverts to *soma* oblivion. John remembers the early days with her when she had sung to him, is greatly moved by his memories, and is exasperated beyond endurance by having the bed surrounded by innumerable identical twins who are being death-conditioned. He strikes one of them in anger, and then Linda dies, the last word on her lips being the name of Popé, and of associations from the past with him rather than with her son. John leaves the room distraught, while the twins are handed chocolate éclairs as part of their conditioning.

gaily-coloured aerial hearses They would naturally form part of the conditioning process – and they contrast markedly with our funeral practice.

a Galloping Senility ward The scourge of tuberculosis which killed off whole areas of the population in the 19th and early 20th centuries was sometimes referred to as 'galloping consumption', a reference to the speed of the disease. Huxley is using the term ironically here.

like fish in an aquarium A highly effective way of indicating that they are in another world – cold-blooded, distant, divorced from reality.

verbena kinds of lemon-scented plant.

flaccid hanging loose or limp, flabby.

a pailful of ordure This is dung, excrement, and note the deliberate use of the image to contrast with the hygienic conditions in the ward.

Bed 20 Sissy Jupe, in Dickens's *Hard Times*, is referred to as Girl Number 20. The world of facts which Dickens so feared has arrived in *Brave New World*.

Chapter 15

John steps out of the lift into the middle of the Delta workers at the Hospital just as their *soma* ration is about to be distributed. He tries to prevent the distribution, appeals to the Deltas to reject it, provokes a riot, and is joined positively by an elated Helmholtz and an embarrassed Bernard. The police are called in and pump *soma* vapour into the air, and the Voice of Reason,

the Voice of Good Feeling, speaks from the Synthetic Music
Box, quelling the disturbance by the 'yearning earnestness' of its
tone. John, Helmholtz and Bernard are arrested.

dolichocephalic long-headed with reference to the skull.
Like maggots . . . This term frequently occurs in John's consciousness
  from now on, since it is the only way he can describe the *disease* of
  mankind itself, the corruption of nature which has taken place.
it was as though a shutter had been opened, a curtain drawn back
  Another image reminiscent of another world, the world of domesticity
  which no longer exists in *Brave New World*.
'Lend me your ears' *Julius Caesar* (Act III Scene ii). The references
  immediately following this seem to be adaptations by John (from
  Shakespeare) in his excitement.
Biarritz A luxury resort on the south-west coast of France.
Mewling and puking From the famous 'All the world's a stage' speech
  in *As You Like It*, Act II Scene vii.
carapace The upper shell of the tortoise and crustaceans.
Ford helps those who help themselves Another adaptation by
  substituting 'Ford' for 'God'.
wambling rolling about in walking, going with an unsteady gait.
valedictions bidding farewells.

Chapter 16

All three are taken before the Controller, Mustapha Mond.
They sink into his luxurious chairs, and he shakes hands with
them. The whole procedure is essentially civilized, though
Bernard is apprehensive and miserable. He is embarrassed by
John's directness and honesty. Mustapha Mond again uses the
history of the past to underline the need for the stability of the
brave new world, with the consequent muzzling of art and
science. He explains his own choice, how he was a very good
scientist but ultimately opted for conformity rather than exile to
an island, knowing that his own abilities could be used in the
control of others. Bernard has to be *soma*-vaporized because of
his reactions to the thought of being sent to an island. Helmholtz
asks to go to the Falkland Islands, and then leaves to see if he can
help Bernard.

The Gamma Butler In 1931, when *Brave New World* was written,
  butlers would still be a feature of upper-class life, and P. G.
  Wodehouse's immortal Jeeves would be enjoying great popularity.
reading-machine bobbins These provide an indication of Huxley

working in depth to get the details of his society in *Brave New World* right.

the Society for the Propagation of Fordian Knowledge The Society for the Promotion of Christian Knowledge was originally founded in 1698. Detroit was, of course, the home of the Ford industries.

'Sometimes a thousand twangling instruments . . . and sometimes voices' Caliban's poetry of utterance, despite his savagery – obvious parallels here with John (*The Tempest*, Act III Scene ii).

'Goats and monkeys' *Othello*, Act IV Scene i.

'they're told by an idiot' An adaptation of Macbeth's speech in Act V Scene v.

'You cannot pour upper-caste champagne surrogate' A clever version of 'You can't pour quarts into pint pots'.

Every discovery in pure science is potentially subversive A statement true for his society and our own, witness the nuclear and atomic discoveries of the age in which we live.

the Corn Dances i.e. ritual dances by the Indians in order to bring about good crops.

all our science is just a cookery book . . . illicit cooking Again the irony is effective because it refers to the domesticity which has disappeared – and it is doubly ironic in the mouth of Mustapha Mond, who in his role as Controller has to make sure that there is no 'illicit cooking'.

'I'm interested in truth . . . I like science. But truth's a menace, science is a public danger' A fine distinction between intellectual appraisal and practical stability; the pursuit of truth, like the pursuit of science, can lead to trouble.

matriarchies Social organization in which the mothers are heads of the families and rule.

The Marquesas These are in French Oceania, inhabited largely by Polynesians. Gauguin painted there, and Melville settled there too.

the Falkland Islands British Crown colony in the South Atlantic, with sheep-breeding and whaling as the main occupations.

Chapter 17

The Controller continues to talk to John, producing some forbidden books like ·*The Imitation of Christ* and *The Varieties of Religious Experience*. He reveals that he has 'A whole collection of pornographic old books' like these. Mond continues that God perhaps exists, but there is no room for him in an age which has chosen 'machinery and medicine and happiness'. The debate centres on the right to feel, the right to experience, with John quoting supportive instances from Shakespeare, and Mond replying with the necessities which make for Community, Identity,

Stability. It is Shakespeare – life and suffering – against the Violent Passion Surrogate, which 'floods the whole system with adrenalin. It's the complete physiological equivalent of fear and rage ... without any of the inconveniences'. John, true to his conditioning among the Indians and by Shakespeare, chooses the right to be unhappy.

The Imitation of Christ Thomas à Kempis (1379–1471), German religious writer; the substance of the book is profoundly pious, elevated and passionate. It was translated into English as early as 1440.

The Varieties of Religious Experience William James (1842–1910) was the elder brother of the distinguished novelist Henry James.

Cardinal Newman (1801–90) Celebrated writer on religion, he doubted the Anglican standpoint and resigned his living at St Mary's Oxford in 1843. He entered the Roman church in 1845, set up the Birmingham Oratory in 1847, wrote *Apologia pro vita sua* in 1864, and was made a Cardinal in 1879.

'I, Pandulph of fair Milan cardinal ...' *King John,* Act III Scene i.

'A man who dreams of fewer things than there are in heaven and earth' A rough approximation to Hamlet's speech in Act I Scene v.

Bradley F. H. Bradley (1846–1924), English idealist philosopher who exerted an influence on Bertrand Russell.

'The Gods are just ... I am here' *King Lear,* Act V Scene iii.

Providence takes its cue from men The Controller argues that the way society organizes itself and establishes its stability is of primary importance; this is what life and fate are all about, rather than the rule of an arbitrary supreme being.

postulates fundamental conditions, prerequisites.

'But value dwells not in particular will ... as in the prizer' *Troilus and Cressida,* Act II Scene ii.

neurasthenia nervous debility.

'If after every tempest comes such calms ... have wakened death' *Othello,* Act II Scene i.

'Whether 'tis nobler ... and by opposing end them' Part of Hamlet's famous soliloquy which begins 'To be or not to be ...' *Hamlet,* Act III Scene i.

'Exposing what is mortal and unsure ...' *Hamlet,* Act IV Scene iv.

adrenalin Hormone secretion which affects circulation and muscular action.

Chapter 18

Bernard – now quite reconciled to his lot – and Helmholtz take their leave of John; they are off to their island, but John has to stay since the Controller wishes to continue with the experiment.

John seeks out an abandoned air-lighthouse and begins to fashion bows and arrows as the beginning of fending for himself, but first of all he scourges himself with a whip. Unfortunately he is seen, and now has to endure the invasion of that privacy – and loneliness – which he cherishes so much. First the *Hourly Radio* disturbs him (he kicks the interviewer), and then Darwin Bonaparte films him, and the sightseers begin to pour in upon him. He rushes at them abusively, sees Lenina, beats her, succumbs to *soma* and 'orgy-porgy'; he wakes the next day, is guilt-ridden, and hangs himself.

Guildford A county town in Surrey, in the Wey valley, with many distinctive historical features.

the Wey valley The river Wey, formed from several branches rising in the Haslemere area, is navigable at Godalming.

Godalming . . . Milford . . . Witley The route and the places mentioned in this paragraph can be readily traced in any gazetteer or map covering the area. There is an interesting running irony in the list given, since many of the places are of historic interest but here are merely location marks on the routes of helicopters.

the Hog's Back Part of the long chalk ridge of the North Downs.

hermitage A significant choice by the author, epitomizing as it does the lonely life which is anathema to the inhabitants of the brave new world.

Claudius See *Hamlet*, Act III Scene iii.

silos Pits or airtight structures in which green crops are pressed and kept for fodder.

like turkey-buzzards, settling on a corpse A vivid image from nature to stress the predatory nature of man, who will seize upon sensation and strip it to the bones; in other words, exploit it without respect.

nocked notched at ends of bows for holding string.

Primo Mellon Fascinating linking of two names, that of Andrew Mellon (1855–1937), American banker, industrial magnate and fiscal reformer; and, perhaps, the 'Primo' is Carnera, Italian heavyweight boxer who won the world title in Huxley's time.

foot-and-mouth baller Again the play on words carries its own irony – 'foot-and-mouth' being a disease of cattle, and perhaps games a 'disease' of man.

coccyx the small triangular bone ending the spinal column in man.

The Fordian Science Monitor An equivalent of the *Christian Science Monitor*.

'Eternity was in our lips and eyes' *Antony and Cleopatra*, Act I Scene iii.

Darwin Bonaparte Another fine combination, this time of Charles Darwin (1809–82), the great English naturalist and biologist who wrote *The Origin of Species* (1859); and Napoleon, surnamed

Bonaparte, great military leader and Emperor of the French, who lived from 1769 until 1821.

the gorillas' wedding A finely satirical touch when one considers public interest in such occasions as chimpanzees' tea-parties at the zoo.

'And all our yesterdays have lighted fools . . .' *Macbeth*, Act V Scene v.

'A good kissing carrion' *Hamlet*, Act II Scene ii.

'As flies to wanton boys . . . they kill us for their sport' *King Lear*, Act IV Scene i.

'Besides thy best of rest is sleep . . . which is no more' *Measure for Measure*, Act III Scene i.

'Perchance to dream . . . in that sleep of death, what dreams' *Hamlet*, Act III Scene i.

Like locusts they came . . . A finely economical image, ironically reminding us of the Old Testament and the plagues of Egypt, when locusts destroyed the crops.

acetate-shantung the latter being soft, undressed Chinese silk.

petits-beurres Small, semi-sweet biscuits.

'We-want-the-whip' The rhythm of the chant, of crowd incantation moving towards frenzy, is seen in the repetition; which in one form or another dates back to Roman times of Christian martyrdom in the Coliseum and perhaps today is seen in the ritual encouragement at football matches.

'Fitchew!' A toad. *Troilus and Cressida*, Act V Scene i.

'Fry, lechery, fry!' *Troilus and Cressida*, Act V Scene ii.

plump incarnation of turpitude 'pneumatic', embodiment of depravity.

two unhurried compass needles . . . A fine climaxing paragraph, for the feet of the dead man swing in all the directions, point to all the corners, of the brave new world which has killed him.

Revision questions on Chapters 14–18

1 Write an account of John's reactions at the Park Lane Hospital for the Dying.

2 Consider the attitude of all three – John, Helmholtz and Bernard – in their interview with Mustapha Mond.

3 What do you learn of Mustapha Mond's attitudes and character during this conversation?

4 How does Huxley create an atmosphere of frustration for John during the final chapter?

5 Give, as clearly as you can, and referring to the text in support, reasons for John's suicide.

The characters

Huxley has sometimes been accused of not creating 'rounded' characters, and indeed in *Brave New World* character is to a degree subordinate to theme, presentation and prophetic or moral comment between the lines. But the characters of the novel are individualized, and it would be doing Huxley a disservice not to give full attention to his portrayals, for they reflect at least facets of personality and, sometimes, more than a hint of complexity or completeness.

Bernard Marx

'It's the alcohol they put in his surrogate.'

Bernard Marx has some complexity, and there is certainly a marked ironic emphasis in the choice of name. Bernard is an Alpha who works in the Psychology Bureau; he has a contempt for the conventional observations of his fellow-workers (witness their praise of the detail in the bearskin rug), and is in love with – contrary to his conditioning – Lenina Crowne. He has all the classic qualities of the outsider: physically stunted in comparison with the other Alphas – this gives him an inferiority complex which occasionally manifests itself aggressively – he has feelings which the others don't have, he has imagination and the wish to experience what is 'different', he is unpopular because of his own difference and, of course, he is vulnerable and feels he is being criticized as, indeed, he often is. Almost by sleight of hand Huxley changes his apparent direction, for we soon learn that he is not the hero of the novel; his human frailty is revealed, and in the words of Helmholtz Watson, he lacks 'pride'. He also lacks nerve and consistency, weakly resorts to *soma* when anything goes wrong, and panics or is abject according to circumstances – witness his reaction to the fact that he had left his eau-de-Cologne tap running in the bathroom or, more particularly, his apprehension at the Savage's outspoken remarks to Mustapha Mond. We should consider also his rather feeble attempts not to become involved when John and Helmholtz are haranguing the

Deltas at the Park Lane Hospital for the Dying. Bernard is inherently weak. Once arrived at the Savage Reservation, and having talked to John and Linda, he acts forthwith with the main chance always in the forefront of his mind. He grows in confidence and importance, writes pompous reports to Mustapha Mond (who takes note and resolves to teach him a lesson later), and then becomes a social-climber and name-dropper doing, in effect, all those things of which he was contemptuous in the past. Thus he exposes the Director – 'Tomakin' – by producing Linda and John publicly; he invites celebrated guests to meet 'Mr Savage' with pretentious affectation, and he 'has' all the girls he wants, including the Headmistress of Eton. But we have noted his weakness much earlier in the narration, for when he hears that the Director has said in public that he (Bernard) is to be exiled to Iceland, his reaction is one of self-pity and incipient hysteria. His inability to rise to the crisis which is the test of character is seen in the long exchanges between himself, John, Helmholtz and Mustapha Mond; Helmholtz's integrity can be set beside Bernard's outburst when he is told that he will be sent to an island: 'You can't send *me*. I haven't done anything. It was the others. I swear it was the others,' and this gives place to the abject, 'Oh please, your fordship, please.' Only a *soma* vaporization can deal with this grovelling, though afterwards Bernard does regain his composure and his sense of loyalty. His face has 'a new expression of determined resignation', and he praises Helmholtz for the sympathy and kindness he has shown him. In Bernard, Huxley explores the nature of a man who wishes not to conform, but who is ultimately reduced by the society in which he lives; from being unwanted he becomes sought after, with the result that he loses his head and takes whatever he can get. Rejected again, and abjectly frightened, he rediscovers that core of sensitivity, his own essential humanity, and accepts his lot.

Lenina Crowne

'Oh, she's a splendid girl. Wonderfully pneumatic. I'm surprised you haven't had her.'

In some ways Lenina approximates to Bernard, although she has little understanding of his motivation when, for instance, he brings the helicopter down low over the waves, or of his reactions when they first arrive at the Savage Reservation. Nor does she understand his apparent unwillingness to 'have' her. But the parallels with him, although she is certainly not an outsider, are there. Fanny has to warn her about her relationship with Henry Foster ('There's been nobody else except Henry all that time. Has there?') and this tendency ('I haven't been feeling very keen on promiscuity lately') becomes an obsession when she has had time to take stock of John. In going to the Savage Reservation with Bernard she has chosen to do the unconventional, but her conditioning is such that she cannot live with physical discomfort, and more particularly the sights and smells of the Indians' lives; the ritual, the initiation of the young boy, the sight of blood – all these make her physically ill, and she is overcome by the grossness, the grotesqueness and ageing of Linda. The contradictions within Lenina are subtly indicated in her name, but essentially she conforms to mass practice when anything becomes uncomfortable and resorts to *soma*. She has a *soma* holiday in reaction against the Reservation, and feeds Bernard and John with hypnopaedic platitudes during their separate outbursts, and always turns her pneumatic charms to the best advantage. The Arch-Community-Songster presents her with a little golden zipper fastening in the form of a T, but although she is able to induce the conventional sexual response in Bernard after he has swallowed sufficient *soma*, John remains inviolable until the very end, for his is a romantic love as distinct from the synthetic sensuality which Lenina invites. She is 'uncommonly pretty', and experiences, in her love for John, all the frustrations of an unconditioned human being or, as Huxley puts it:

all the sensations normally experienced at the beginning of a Violent Passion Surrogate treatment – a sense of dreadful emptiness, a breathless apprehension, a nausea. Her heart seemed to stop beating.

Fanny's advice, coupled with *soma*, leads her to attempt the seduction of John, but she receives a good slap for her pains ('she could see the imprint of an open hand standing out distinct and crimson on the pearly flesh'). In the final degrading sequence she is beaten by John, but he takes *soma* and abandons himself to her. The fact that she has natural emotions up to a point makes Lenina interesting, and she is capable too of human error – witness her failure to give the sleeping-sickness injection to the Alpha-minus embryo. She represents the fact that scientific conditioning lacks absoluteness, its success can never be fully assured, since human nature and human reaction can be controlled but not stifled.

Helmholtz Watson

'... this admirable committee man and best mixer had realized quite suddenly that sport, women, communal activities were only, as far as he was concerned, second-best ... Really, and at the bottom, he was interested in something else.'

Helmholtz Watson is an Alpha-Plus, a good friend to Bernard, sympathetic if a little contemptuous of his friend's weakness; he is a lecturer in the College of Emotional Engineering and writes for the *Hourly Radio*, composes feely scenarios and produces suitable slogans for the industry of conditioning. He has everything that should make for conformity and stability – physique, sporting ability, is an 'indefatigable lover' – but he is, in the words of his contemporaries, 'too able'. His combination of very high intelligence and sensitivity leads him to explore, in a poem which contrasts with the hypnopaedic rubbish he has to write, the prospect of loneliness; this is, of course, treason to the current régime. He is in trouble but, unlike Bernard, he is equal to the situation. He takes immediately to John (much to Bernard's jealous annoyance) and listens elatedly to his readings from Shakespeare, though at times his own conditioning causes him to laugh uproariously, for example at the sexual morality of *Romeo and Juliet*. Although he has pride he is not above apologizing, but his salient characteristic is his integrity; in the conversation with Mustapha Mond following his (Helmholtz's) arrest when he has come to the aid of John in the Park Lane Hospital for the Dying, he remains balanced, civilized, understanding fully what he has done and being determined to stick by it. He chooses the Falkland Islands for his exile, preferring a testing climate in which to establish his own capacity to experience the physical and emotional extremes outside the cushioning effects of *soma*. He takes Mustapha Mond's point that he will be happier there, with a selected group of radicals and outsiders, than he would be in the conditioned society in which he has already plumbed his frustrations. He too demonstrates that no conditioning can be perfect, for human nature triumphs in Helmholtz despite the pressures of his position. He represents therefore an affirmation of optimism, of the capacity of the human frame to take drugs and conditioning and still retain its individual instinct for response and decision. Helmholtz has pride and will-power; his own decision is in contrast to that of Mustapha Mond in the past for he chooses the island, whereas Mond chose the direct road to promotion and executive conformity.

Mustapha Mond

'I'm the head cook now. But I was an inquisitive young scullion once. I started doing a bit of cooking on my own. Unorthodox cooking. A bit of real science, in fact.'

Once more we find the intriguing nature of the names (see the chapter notes on p.34 for the hypothetical associations), and Mustapha Mond is important not merely because of his position but because of the significance of his two appearances in the story. The first is when he talks to the students who are being shown round the conditioning rooms by the Director; here his role is functional, since he fills in for us – and the students – the historical gaps which bring us up to AF 632. Perhaps the most marked feature of his conduct here is the fact that he is apparently oblivious to the flattery and sycophantic attentions of the D.H.C. Later, he receives Bernard's reports on the 'Savage' and Linda, and gives permission for them to be brought to London. Thereafter he gives Bernard enough rope metaphorically to hang himself, stepping in only after the arrests. His discussions with John and with Helmholtz provide one of the most interesting sections of the novel, and he reveals his own temptations and tendencies in the past. Mond is a psychologically integrated character, convincing and fuller than one is initially led to expect. He has much in common with Helmholtz and he has a positive knowledge of the past, having in his possession such forbidden gems as the Bible and *The Imitation of Christ*, and he knows, for example, the views of Cardinal Newman. But in that past he had to choose, and he chose to survive and conform, aware of the fact that his own high abilities would ensure that he would direct the conformity of others. He is enlightened enough to know that radicals and outsiders put on the other rights which John chooses to enjoy.

John – the Savage

The blood rushed up into the young man's face; he dropped his eyes, raised them again for a moment only to find her still smiling at him, and was so much overcome that he had to turn away and pretend to be looking very hard at something on the other side of the square.

I have given the above quotation in full because it exemplifies the sensitivity of John. He is easily the most sympathetic character in *Brave New World*, for everything he does and says is based on feeling, and not self-indulgent feeling. It is perhaps true that the final sequence which has him returning to nature, living in a lighthouse, and making himself bows and arrows, is somewhat too self-consciously symbolic to be convincing, but his reactions to Lenina, to Bernard, to Linda and to Helmholtz carry the undeniable ring of truth. He represents the summit of Huxley's ironic achievement, for as a Savage he shows himself to be more civilized emotionally than those whose conditioning has taught them only to take and consume and not to give. John is jealous of his mother's love for Popé, bewildered by her own rejection of him, ostracized by the Indians at the time of ritualistic initiation, but deeply imbued with guilt and a sense of inadequacy, a sense too of religious fervour and the need to purge oneself of wickedness and corruption and temptation. He is the Noble Savage, reared on Shakespeare and also 'Bye, Baby Banting, soon you'll need decanting', but in the warmth and filth of intimacy and not by the hypnopaedic microphone. His inheritance is a rich one, for he can identify with Othello, with Lear, with Macbeth and, when he sees Lenina, with Romeo. He is delighted at the thought of going to the 'other place' and perhaps finds Miranda's words suitable to his own state – she loving Ferdinand, he loving Lenina, and the 'mankind' each sees being 'beauteous' as a result. But his sensitivity, his emotionalism, his idealism and sense of moral rightness, all are affronted by the brave new world in which he finds himself. Sickened by the physical uniformity of machine-working Bokanovskified twins, sickened by sexual promiscuity, sickened above all by the total lack of humanity and the addiction to *soma* he sees about everywhere, John revolts and tries to preach – and I think that is the right word – reason to a group of Delta workers unable to do without their *soma* ration. Arrested and taken before Mustapha Mond, having first found a kindred spirit in Helmholtz, he defiantly maintains his right to be unhappy, but his own tragedy is that he is not sent to an island. Mond decides to continue the experiment, and the Savage retreats to a lighthouse where, after some peace, he is threatened by sightseers after a film has been made which shows him whipping himself; this is considered whimsical to the point of humour by those who seek him out. He beats Lenina, who is in the van of the sightseers, but succumbs to temptation in the form of *soma* and Lenina, and awakes the next morning after 'orgy-porgy', so driven to desperation by his sense of sin that he hangs himself. He represents natural man overcome, defeated by science which provides the wherewithal of living without the freedom to choose how one wants to live.

Other characters

None of the other characters is major enough to merit detailed examination, although they are interesting in the glimpses we have of them, and with some a particular facet of personality is developed. The D.H.C. is one such example, with a hint of depth to his character. At first he is the complacent representative of authority, somewhat blasé, showing the students with some pride how things are done in terms of conditioning, but he slips into the background with the arrival of Mustapha Mond, to whom he devotes his sycophantic attentions, being determined to please:

'Go away, little girl,' shouted the D.H.C. angrily. 'Go away, little boy! Can't you see his fordship's busy? Go and do your erotic play somewhere else.'

He reveals his own experience of twenty-five years earlier at the New Mexico Reservation to Bernard, sharply criticizes Bernard when he realizes what he has said, and determines to punish him later by sending him to Iceland. Filled with magisterial platitudes he prepares the public denouncement, but the tables are dramatically turned on 'Tomakin' when Linda and then John appear. He takes a permanent *soma* holiday. It is a natural association to move from the D.H.C. to *Linda* ('The blotched and sagging face twitched grotesquely into the grimace of extreme grief'). Physically aged and fat, her conditioning has lasted inwardly but not outwardly; finding herself forsaken in the Reservation by Tomakin, she 'naturally' reverts to the only way of life she knows – promiscuity. As a result she is beaten by the Indian women since she has taken their men; has to make do with *mescal* instead of *soma*; becomes a mother and alternately rejects and loves John because of her early conditioning; loves Popé rather more than the other men; and treasures her memories of the 'other place' with its cleanliness and sterilization. She is regarded as a grotesque joke when she does appear, though she provides an area of research interest for Dr Shaw, who keeps her on the *soma* which she has craved for so long until the doses finally kill her. We remember that she was only a Beta-minus, and that her conditioning had always caused her to be divided in herself. Linda is a simple sensualist, and *soma* gives her the dreams of ecstasy which her decaying flesh can no longer provide.

The rest of the characters are indisputably minor. Admittedly *Henry Foster*, as the bright young executive – does he succeed to the D.H.C.'s position? – registers because of his knowledgeability not only about conditioning but about phosphorous reclamation, and he has all the smugness of conformity which is needed to be successful. *Fanny Crowne* represents conformity as well, being, in effect, Lenina's good angel and warning her of the need to be seen to be practising promiscuity. The *Warden of the Reservation* is a sub-standard Henry Foster, full of directions, information, controls – a limited administrator as befits someone in charge of an unpleasant area. *Popé* and *Mitsima*, the old man who instructs John, come fitfully alive in John's recollections, but they are vivid and real if only momentarily. In the brave new world there is the good-natured, sex-hormone chewing-gum conditioned *Benito Hoover*; the ironically named and willowy *Miss Keate*, Headmistress of Eton; the suave and self-important and sensual *Arch-Community-Songster*; the coccyx-kicked *Primo Mellon* and that intrepid big-game photographer *Darwin Bonaparte*. None is dull, all contribute to the action, whether the brush-stroke which made them is light or heavy. Huxley has a wonderful eye for idiosyncratic human behaviour, and all his characters, however minor, reflect this.

General questions plus questions on related topics for coursework/examinations on other books you may be studying

1 Write an essay on the main aspects of Huxley's style in Brave New World.

Suggested notes for essay answer:

You should refer closely to the text – quote wherever possible – and include mention and examination of some or all of the following: *psychological* integration of character (John and childhood – the consciousness); the *allusive* writing of the novel, from characters' names to literary and a wide range of cultural references. Single out particularly the use of *Shakespeare*: link this perhaps with the running *irony*. Mention scientific allusion, cliché, colloquialisms, parody, satire, humour and the particular range of speech mannerisms. Proverbial sayings and song would obviously be included. The range of *imagery* should be examined, and some indication of its effects should be indicated.

2 Indicate the range of Huxley's satire on his own society in the novel.

3 With which character do you sympathize most in *Brave New World*?

4 What aspects of scientific discovery seem to you most frightening in *Brave New World*?

5 How far have Huxley's prophecies been realized since the publication of this novel? You should refer closely to the text in your answer.

6 Write an essay in general appreciation of the literary qualities of *Brave New World*.

7 From your own reading of *Brave New World*, indicate what aspects of life are important and worth preserving for Huxley.

8 What contribution does Huxley's learning make to our appreciation of *Brave New World*?

9 Which scene in *Brave New World* do you find most moving, and why?

10 In what ways is Aldous Huxley an entertaining writer?

11 Compare *Brave New World* with any other Utopian or anti-Utopian work you have read.

12 What does Huxley's use of Shakespeare contribute to our appreciation of *Brave New World*?

13 Give an account of a book you have read which deals with events in the future.

14 In *Brave New World, soma* is a drug. Write about a book you have read where drugs have some influence on the action.

15 Indicate the part played by scientific discovery and practice in your chosen book.

16 In what ways does a book you have read recently reflect social and class differences in society?

17 Describe a situation in one of your books where an individual is persecuted because of his views or his behaviour.

18 Describe an attractive yet selfish character in one of your books.

19 Write about the presentation of the media – press, film, television – in a book you know well.

20 Discuss the conflict between rational and emotional behaviour in any book you have read recently.

Brodie's Notes

TITLES IN THE SERIES

Jane Austen	**Pride and Prejudice**
Robert Bolt	**A Man for All Seasons**
Emily Brontë	**Wuthering Heights**
Charlotte Brontë	**Jane Eyre**
Geoffrey Chaucer	**Prologue to the Canterbury Tales**
Geoffrey Chaucer	**The Nun's Priest's Tale**
Geoffrey Chaucer	**The Wife of Bath's Tale**
Geoffrey Chaucer	**The Pardoner's Prologue and Tale**
Charles Dickens	**Great Expectations**
Gerald Durrell	**My Family and Other Animals**
T. S. Eliot	**Selected Poems**
George Eliot	**Silas Marner**
F. Scott Fitzgerald	**The Great Gatsby and Tender is the Night**
E. M. Forster	**A Passage to India**
John Fowles	**The French Lieutenant's Woman**
Anne Frank	**The Diary of Anne Frank**
William Golding	**Lord of the Flies**
Graham Handley (ed)	**The Metaphysical Poets: John Donne to Henry Vaughan**
Thomas Hardy	**Far From the Madding Crowd**
Thomas Hardy	**Tess of the D'Urbervilles**
Thomas Hardy	**The Mayor of Casterbridge**
Aldous Huxley	**Brave New World**
John Keats	**Selected Poems and Letters of John Keats**
Philip Larkin	**Selected Poems of Philip Larkin**
D. H. Lawrence	**Sons and Lovers**
Laurie Lee	**Cider with Rosie**
Harper Lee	**To Kill a Mockingbird**
Arthur Miller	**The Crucible**
Arthur Miller	**Death of a Salesman**
George Orwell	**1984**
George Orwell	**Animal Farm**
J. B. Priestley	**An Inspector Calls**
J. D. Salinger	**The Catcher in the Rye**
William Shakespeare	**The Merchant of Venice**
William Shakespeare	**King Lear**
William Shakespeare	**A Midsummer Night's Dream**
William Shakespeare	**Twelfth Night**
William Shakespeare	**Hamlet**
William Shakespeare	**As You Like It**
William Shakespeare	**Romeo and Juliet**
William Shakespeare	**Julius Caesar**
William Shakespeare	**Macbeth**
William Shakespeare	**Antony and Cleopatra**
William Shakespeare	**Othello**
William Shakespeare	**The Tempest**

George Bernard Shaw	**Pygmalion**
Alan Sillitoe	**Selected Fiction**
John Steinbeck	**Of Mice and Men** and **The Pearl**
Alice Walker	**The Color Purple**

ENGLISH COURSEWORK BOOKS

Terri Apter	**Women and Society**
Kevin Dowling	**Drama and Poetry**
Philip Gooden	**Conflict**
Philip Gooden	**Science Fiction**
Margaret K. Gray	**Modern Drama**
Graham Handley	**Modern Poetry**
Graham Handley	**Prose**
Graham Handley	**Childhood and Adolescence**
R. J. Sims	**The Short Story**